THE

FRANKPLEDGE SYSTEM

BY

WILLIAM ALFRED MORRIS, Ph.D.

ASSISTANT PROFESSOR OF EUROPEAN HISTORY IN THE UNIVERSITY
OF WASHINGTON

LONGMANS, GREEN, AND CO.

FOURTH AVENUE & 30TH STREET, NEW YORK

LONDON, BOMBAY, AND CALCUTTA

1910

THE UNIVERSITY PRESS, CAMBRIDGE, U. S. A.

TO THE MEMORY OF

PROFESSOR CHARLES GROSS

IS DEDICATED THIS WORK

UNDERTAKEN THROUGH HIS INSPIRATION

AND COMPLETED UNDER HIS GUIDANCE

PREFACE

No writer has hitherto made a study of frankpledge except in a very few of its aspects. From 1832, the date of Palgrave's *Rise and Progress of the English Commonwealth*, down to the publication of Maitland's *Select Pleas in Manorial and other Seignorial Courts* in 1889, interest was almost exclusively centred in questions relating to the time and place of the origin of the system and to its supposed importance in the communal organization of Saxon England. Maitland's investigation as to its place in the tourn and leet system, published in the above-named volume, opened up a new field by emphasizing the real constitutional significance of the institution; and in the last twenty years there has been published and made easily accessible much material illustrating the procedure of the various medieval English courts that had to do with frankpledge, and thus affording a view of the system in operation. Only one person, however, has attempted to make such a study of the workings of the system as its importance demands, and even his investigation is limited in range to a local field, the city of Norwich; but the excellence and interest of this work (Hudson's *Leet Jurisdiction in Norwich*, published some seventeen years ago) encourage the undertaking of a similar study of the institution wherever found in England. One might well wish that Liebermann, the latest and most accurate scholar to write upon frankpledge, had been able to turn his great learning in this direction; but he has, like earlier writers, concerned himself chiefly with questions touching the beginnings, rather than the workings, of the system. It has been the aim of the present writer, without neglecting the information already so well brought out concerning both the origin of frankpledge and its constitutional importance as part of the local government system, to make a study of its maintenance, functions, and decline, and also to discover just how far it is possible at this time to tell where it existed in England and where it did not exist.

Although a list of books used in preparing the following chapters will be found on a later page, something may be said here as to the importance of some of the more prominent ones, and as to the writer's indebtedness to them. The sources for the origin of frankpledge are the Anglo-Saxon laws, and the Anglo-Norman compilations known as the *Leges Henrici Primi*,[1] the *Leges Edwardi Confessoris*, and the various versions of the so-called laws of William the Conqueror. The splendidly edited *Gesetze*, issued by Liebermann within the past twelve years, contains laws not before published, and clearly supersedes the earlier work of Thorpe and Schmid in this field. Of the older works on frankpledge Palgrave's is the best. His conclusions, although sometimes conjectural, have remained to the present time the basis of information in regard to the distribution of the system; and in some ways they almost anticipate Liebermann's investigations. Kemble, who wrote his *Saxons in England* (1849) under the spell of the mark theory, uncritically assumed the existence of frankpledge in Saxon England, and attempted to make the frankpledge tithing a unit of local organization. A little later, William Maurer, in his *Inquiry into Anglo-Saxon Mark Courts*, made further arguments along

---

[1] Throughout the present work the abbreviated title *Leges Henrici* is used for *Leges Henrici Primi*.

the same line, although Marquardsen had in 1852 shown in a
convincing manner that frankpledge could not have existed
beside the *borh* system found in the Anglo-Saxon laws. Marquardsen's work is still the most detailed study of the Anglo-
Saxon surety system in print; but Waitz reaches very much the
same conclusions in summarizing the literature on the subject
in his *Deutsche Verfassungsgeschichte*. It was in the latter work
that the similarity between frankpledge and English institutions
known to have been introduced by the Norman kings was first
clearly set forth. Another distinct contribution of Waitz lay in
proving that frankpledge was not a primitive Germanic institution. Waitz is, however, too much inclined to hold that the
frankpledge tithing was a creation of William the Conqueror
rather than a development of Saxon usage. Schmid, in editing
Die Gesetze der Angelsachsen, first adduced the argument for a
Saxon origin of frankpledge from the ignorance of writers of the
twelfth century; and Liebermann has more recently sought to
strengthen the same line of thought. The contribution of Stubbs
to the literature of frankpledge lay in pointing out that, although
the similarity of the obligation of the tithing to that of the hundred in cases of murder points very clearly to William the Conqueror as the organizer of the system, frankpledge is nevertheless to be regarded as a development of Anglo-Saxon suretyship.
Maitland, who believed that the origin of the institution is in
large measure yet to be explained, never undertook to grapple
with the problem, but merely dropped here and there in his
writings hints that seemed of value to him. He adopted the
theory of a Saxon origin. Liebermann, in attempting to show
in his *Ueber die Leges Edwardi Confessoris* that frankpledge
came into existence at some time between 1030 and 1066, depends much upon the ideas of persons who wrote after 1115;
but his scholarly conclusions as to conditions between 1030 and

1086 are strongly in favor of dating the beginning of the system from the reign of the Conqueror.

Concerning the distribution of frankpledge, the *Rotuli Hundredorum* and the *Placita de Quo Warranto* contain valuable material which has not before been utilized. The recently published *Pipe Rolls* from the fifth year of Henry II onward, taken with the *Pipe Roll* for the first year of Richard I long ago edited by Hunter, and the *Pipe Rolls* for Staffordshire published by the William Salt Archaeological Society, give a considerable body of material, not easily available before, which illustrates the distribution and working of frankpledge in the twelfth century. The various judicial and municipal records also enable one to trace the system, and thus to check, and to a certain extent to correct, the conclusions of Palgrave.

The works that best illustrate the working of the system in the municipalities are, besides Hudson's *Leet Jurisdiction in Norwich* already noticed, the *Records of the Borough of Leicester* edited by the late Miss Bateson, *Oxford City Documents* edited by Rogers, Stevenson's *Records of the Borough of Nottingham*, and the *Records of the Borough of Northampton* edited by Markham and Cox. For London, Riley's edition of muniments in the Rolls Series is valuable. Some material on frankpledge in the boroughs is also to be found in the *Rotuli Hundredorum* and the *Placita de Quo Warranto*. Of secondary works on the boroughs that of Merewether and Stephens is most serviceable. Pollock and Maitland's *History of English Law* contains an excellent but brief summary of the municipal frankpledge system.

The most important class of material for the study of the real operation of frankpledge is, as hinted above, the court rolls, especially the assize rolls. The writer has been able to verify his conclusions from this class of printed records by an examination of a considerable number of the manuscripts in the

Public Record Office. Toward making this kind of material on frankpledge available Maitland has done more than any one else. His *Pleas of the Crown for the County of Gloucester* and his *Select Pleas of the Crown* are especially valuable as showing how the royal justices supervised and made use of the system. Of equal importance are the *Somersetshire Pleas*, edited by Healey for the Somerset Record Society, and a similar collection of pleas for Staffordshire published by the Salt Archaeological Society. On the manorial side of frankpledge, Maitland's *Select Pleas in Manorial Courts*, Hone's *Manor and Manorial Records*, and Bickley's extracts from the court rolls of Dulwich manor (published in Young's *History of Dulwich College*) are the best printed collections, although there is a wealth of material scattered through many manorial court rolls. The law as to view of frankpledge is given by Bracton, and in the legal compilations of the time of Edward I known as Britton and Fleta. On the manorial view of frankpledge the *Court Baron*, edited by Maitland and Baildon, is invaluable. The work done by Maitland on the origin of leet procedure, and published in the introduction to his *Select Pleas in Manorial Courts*, has revolutionized old theories as to the antiquity of the leet. It has, however, been supplemented lately by Hearnshaw's *Leet Jurisdiction in England*.

The part of the work upon which it has been most difficult to find information is the decline of frankpledge; for in the fourteenth century, when specially assigned justices superseded the old justices in eyre as the trial judges in criminal pleas, the changed form of record did not mention the suretyship responsibility of the tithing. Occasional cases in the *Year Books* are of service here, as are also some works of the fifteenth and sixteenth centuries, among them Lambard's *Duties of Constables*, Powell's *Antiquity of the Leet*, and Kitchin's *Court Leete and*

Court Baron. After the failure of the assize rolls, however, the principal sources for this late period of frankpledge history are the manorial court records. Although the writer has been able to examine a good many of these in manuscript, no one can realize better than he how great is the probability that valuable information in regard to the later history of frankpledge lies hidden away in rolls which have not come to his attention. He can but hope that he has discovered the typical facts and cases which they present.

The personal obligations of the writer throughout the time spent in the preparation of this study have been numerous. Above all he is indebted to his master, Professor Charles Gross of Harvard University, whose loss he has just been called to mourn in common with the world of historical scholarship. Professor Gross gave painstaking attention to this work at all stages; his wide acquaintance with medieval English records and his long experience in the art of research were brought to the writer's aid with characteristic generosity; and in the days of his failing strength he devoted to the reading of the proof sheets his usual scrupulous care. Dean Haskins and Professor Merriman have also read the work in proof, and made numerous suggestions from which it has profited. Professor Vinogradoff of Oxford has shown a kindly interest in the work, and through Professor Gross made useful suggestions concerning matters connected with the origin of frankpledge. Mr. George Unwin of London has shown the same interest and the same willingness to aid. The writer gratefully acknowledges the uniform courtesy which he has met with at the hands of the officials of the Public Record Office and of the British Museum. In the preparation of the manuscript his wife has constantly aided him; and to the reading and very helpful criticism of parts of it his friend Professor F. M. Padelford of the University of Washington has devoted time which under the pressure of his numerous duties he could ill afford to spend. A number of friends in Cambridge have given valuable assistance, among them in particular Mr. L. R. Wells, Dr. H. L. Gray, and Dr. F. A. Golder. To Miss A. F. Rowe the writer is under special obligation for verifying references to books cited in the footnotes of the first two chapters, to Dr. Golder for directing the work of verifying those in the remaining chapters.

WILLIAM A. MORRIS.

DECEMBER, 1909.

CONTENTS

CHAPTER I

ORIGIN OF FRANKPLEDGE

CHAPTER II

DISTRIBUTION OF FRANKPLEDGE

CHAPTER III

ORGANIZATION AND FUNCTIONS OF FRANKPLEDGE

CHAPTER IV

VIEW OF FRANKPLEDGE

CHAPTER V

DECLINE AND RESULTS OF THE FRANKPLEDGE SYSTEM

APPENDICES

THE FRANKPLEDGE SYSTEM

CHAPTER I

ORIGIN OF FRANKPLEDGE

THE use of suretyship in some form has characterized legal procedure from ancient times. Before the dawn of European history the system was already connected with civil process and with commercial as well as with criminal law. The present study has to do with this last-named phase of suretyship, which originated in early tribal custom, was retained as society advanced, and has in practically all stages of civilization served as a device to insure the appearance of law-breakers at trial. Although in the Middle Ages the plan was familiar to Germanic nations in general, it is probable that no people has, in the process of developing its legal institutions, followed more diverse modes of pledging in the interest of the public peace than have the Anglo-Saxons. Certainly no more highly centralized and thoroughgoing scheme of suretyship to secure order was ever devised on European soil than that which existed in medieval England under the name of frankpledge.

A definition of frankpledge is given by the earliest writer who attempts to describe the institution. "It is of this sort," says this twelfth-century scribe, "namely, that all men in every vill of the whole realm were by custom under obligation to be (*debebant*) in the suretyship of ten,[1] so that if one of the ten

---

[1] Or, more correctly, of a tithing. See *Leges Edwardi Confessoris*, xx, in Liebermann, *Gesetze*, i. 645; Thorpe, *Ancient Laws*, i. 450; Schmid, *Gesetze*, 502.

commit an offence the nine have him to justice."[1] Frank-pledge, then, was a system of compulsory, collective bail, fixed for individuals not after their arrest for crime but as a safe-guard in anticipation of it.

The name frankpledge, like the institution itself, first ap-pears in the second decade of the twelfth century. The desig-nation employed by the compiler of the *Leges Henrici*, the earliest authority on the subject, is the Latin form *plegium liberale*,[2] the literal translation of which into the Norman-French *franc plege*[3] becomes the origin of the ordinary English name. It was long the belief of scholars that the contemporary twelfth-century English name was *frithborg* (peace-pledge); but Liebermann has discovered that the au-thority of the older manuscripts is in favor of *friborg* (for *freoborg*, free-pledge), the exact etymological equivalent of the Latin and French terms.[4] The earliest name for frankpledge is almost certainly the old English one, for the early Norman writers have no distinctly French designation for it. Gneist undoubtedly gives the correct explanation when he suggests that the word "belongs more to the popular language than to the laws."[5] The term seems not to have originated from the fact that those in frankpledge were legally held to be free men;[6] it belongs rather to that period in late Anglo-Saxon

---

[1] *Leges Edw. Conf.*, xx. 1, in Liebermann, *Gesetze*, i. 645.

[2] *Leges Henrici*, viii. 2, *ibid.* 554; Schmid, *Gesetze*, 441; Thorpe, *Laws*, i. 515.

[3] French *Leis Willelme*, xx. 3a, in Liebermann, *Gesetze*, i. 506.

[4] *Ibid.* 645, ii. 81. In his *Ueber die Leges Edw. Conf.*, 29, he shows that the corruption of *friborg* is easily explained both from the significance of the term and from its form; since the object of the arrangement was peace, since *frith* may, in addition to much else, signify the union of police and mutual re-sponsibility, and since a Frenchman could not utter the *th* sound.

[5] " 'Francplegium' is the Norman translation in the official vernacular of the times" (*English Constitution*, 151, note).

[6] Liebermann (*Ueber die Leges Edw. Conf.*, 82) seems to incline toward this explanation; but almost any other form of pledging might have been called frankpledge for exactly the same reason.

history when the "free engagement of neighbour for neighbour" began to supersede the compulsory suretyship both of the lord for the dependent and of the kindred for the clansman.[1]

Historical accuracy demands an insistence that no kind of suretyship be called frankpledge unless it be clearly the one already described. The distinction between pledge and frankpledge is vital. No amount of tempting speculation upon etymological or institutional origins can obliterate the line between the peculiar mutual pledging of the groups of ten and all other forms. An error common to older writers is to read *friborg* (*frithborg*) into the Anglo-Saxon laws wherever *borg* (*borh*, surety) occurs, and thus to assume the existence of frankpledge a century or so before the institution is ever mentioned.[2] Any reference to a frankpledge system before the Norman Conquest must, however, in the absence of further evidence than that now obtainable, be regarded as misleading.[3] Misapprehension has also arisen from the confusion of frankpledge with forms of suretyship that were undoubtedly contemporary, such as ordinary bail,[4] and mainpast, or the compulsory pledging by the lord for the servant whom he received. The latter

[1] See Green, *Conquest of England*, 229; also below, p. 25, note 3.

[2] This tendency begins with the *leges* of the twelfth century. See the translation of the *Leis* of the Conqueror, ch. xxv (of about the year 1200), in Liebermann, *Gesetze*, i. 511.

[3] Although Vinogradoff (*Growth of the Manor*, 198) says that in the period of the last kings of English and Danish race the government introduced "a system of personal frankpledge," the present writer cannot but feel that the expression is unfortunate. Since only one definite system is ever designated as frankpledge, and since that one is not mentioned until the twelfth century, the propriety of referring to the transitional surety system of an earlier century by that name is more than doubtful.

[4] Farrer (*Lancashire Pipe Rolls*, 91, note) mistakenly says of three men, fined on account of a fourth whom they had pledged, that they were sureties according to the laws of frankpledge. Lord John Hervey, in his *Extracts from the Hundred Rolls of Suffolk* (pp. 77, 119), has even translated the word *replegiari* "that he might be restored to frankpledge."

system was, to be sure, closely connected with frankpledge from its beginnings, and was sometimes even loosely called frankpledge by writers of the twelfth and thirteenth centuries;[1] but in practice the two forms of suretyship were clearly distinct.[2]

The origin of the frankpledge tithing, or group of ten, with the compulsory responsibility of its members for each other has been variously attributed to the Romans, the primitive Germans, the Anglo-Saxons, and the Anglo-Normans. The theory of a Roman origin advanced by both Coote[3] and Finlason[4] depends, like their assumptions in general concerning Roman influence on English institutions, merely on analogy. When one finds that the development of a Saxon *borh* system did not begin till some five centuries after there could have been any direct Roman influence, and recalls the grave doubts generally entertained as to whether any such influence was possible even during the Saxon conquest of Britain, one need give no further attention to this theory.

---

[1] Since suretyship of the lord for the dependent was the characteristic form of Saxon pledging from the tenth century on, and since this variety of *borh* was still to be found in the Norman period, when *friborg* was the prevailing mode, the danger of reading the later form into earlier conditions becomes all the greater. It is a copyist of the *Leges Edwardi*, apparently writing between 1140 and 1159, who first makes *friborg* (*frithborg*) an equivalent for *borh*, describing servants as in the former kind of suretyship (*Leges Edw. Conf.*, xxi, in Liebermann, *Gesetze*, i. 647). According to a translation of about 1200, a French law requiring the lord to have his serving-men in his *plege* reads that he shall have them in *francplegio* (Pseudo-Ingulf version of the *Leis Willelme*, lii, *ibid.* 519). Half a century later Bracton (*De Legibus*, Rolls Series, fol. 124 b, ii. 304, 306) adopts the loose terminology of the copyist of the *Leges Edwardi* by speaking in one passage of the suretyship of servants as frankpledge, though in another he shows that the alternative for every man is either frankpledge or mainpast.

[2] As shown by the familiar entry in court rolls, "non in franco plegio nec de manupastu." The *Leges Henrici* (ch. viii. 2, 2a, in Liebermann, *Gesetze*, i. 554) and the Assize of Clarendon (ch. x, in Stubbs, *Select Charters*, 144) distinctly contrast the two.

[3] *Romans of Britain*, 331–342.

[4] In his Introduction to Reeves's *History of English Law*, p. xlvi, note 3.

The view that the collective suretyship of the tithing was a common Germanic institution [1] has been refuted by Waitz,[2] who shows that in the codes of the various Germanic peoples there is no word either for tithing (*decenna*) or for the head man of a tithing (*decennus*). While the latter is a perfectly familiar figure in English records, the Visigothic and the Frankish *decenus* was respectively a military commander and an overseer of the property of king or nobles, and the Lombard *deganus* was a police officer.[3] No one of them was connected with any village or local community.

The question that remains to be decided is, then, whether the institution which is the subject of this study first appeared in England in the Anglo-Saxon or in the Norman period, a point upon which there is naturally a difference of opinion; for, in the absence of direct, reliable evidence, writers on the subject have been forced to draw inferences from a few scanty facts. Frankpledge suretyship is first mentioned in England half a century after the Norman Conquest. What appears to have been its earliest name is a pure Anglo-Saxon word, but one not to be found before the days of Norman rule. Nowhere do the Anglo-Norman legal writers say that the system, for which the English people retain their own word,[4] is an Anglo-Saxon institution;[5] but, as will appear later, some of them assume this as a fact. Domesday Book has no word for tithing and no mention of frankpledge, for as a financial survey it was

[1] This view is advanced by Möser, Rogge, and Eichorn. See Maurer, in *Kritische Ueberschau*, i. 87.

[2] *Deutsche Verfassungsgeschichte*, i. 458–462.

[3] Mention of this official led some of the older English writers to suppose that frankpledge was imported into England from Lombardy. See *Manchester Leet Records* (Chetham Soc.), prefatory chapter, p. 3, note 1.

[4] "Quam Angli vocant friborgas": *Leges Edw. Conf.*, xx, in Liebermann, *Gesetze*, i. 645.

[5] Schmid, *Gesetze*, 647.

not concerned with the question of suretyship.[1] The Saxon charters in the *Codex Diplomaticus* make no reference to the system, nor do the Norman charters from William I to Henry I seem to contain any allusion to frankpledge or to view of frankpledge. In vain does one look for enlightenment in any known record prior to the twelfth century. The rise of the institution belongs to the vast domain of unrecorded legal development.

The definite medieval statements concerning the rise of frankpledge prove to be but traditions founded on inference. William of Malmesbury, the first of the chroniclers to mention the system, says in his *Gesta Regum*, written a little before 1125,[2] that King Alfred originated the suretyship tithing as well as the hundred.[3] This assertion is, however, the merest conjecture, accepted by no reliable modern authority, and apparently due to an old-time tendency to explain institutional beginnings by a single act of some great lawgiver. What William really does is to have Alfred put every Englishman in the suretyship of a tithing two generations before Alfred's descendant, Edgar, made the finding of suretyship of any kind obligatory upon all freemen. William's statement seems to be the basis of a similar error in the thirteenth century; for the notoriously inaccurate *Mirror of Justices*, which was compiled in London probably between 1285 and 1290, represents Alfred as the founder of many English institutions, including view of frankpledge.[4] The same opinion seems also to have been generally accepted by lawyers of the period; for in the quo warranto pleas of Edward I the king's attorneys set up the theory that view of frankpledge was a right vested in the crown by the con-

---

[1] Schmid, *Gesetze*, 648; Liebermann, *Ueber die Leges Edw. Conf.*, 81, note 1.
[2] See Stubbs's Introduction to the *Gesta Regum* (Rolls Series), i. p. xix.
[3] *Ibid.* 129–130.
[4] Selden Society edition, p. 9.

quest of England,[1] the king, as will be seen later, being content
to leave this franchise in the hands of those who could show
continuous seisin by their ancestors from the time of Richard I.
Even in these pleas, claims to view of frankpledge based on
charters prior to 1190 were not admitted in court, for the reason
that the right was never conveyed specifically, but was merely
read into some vague or general expression.[2] So far as the quo
warranto records show, the royal attorney's theory that view
of frankpledge came down from Saxon times was never sustained against the criticism of this same attorney when it was
advanced by a claimant to the franchise. The legend that
Alfred was the founder of the frankpledge system had, nevertheless, become fixed in English legal tradition, and was perpetuated in legal works as late as the seventeenth century.[3]

Of far greater value are the conclusions of modern authorities; and yet opinion is still well-nigh hopelessly divided between those who hold that frankpledge was an Anglo-Saxon
institution and those who believe that it had its rise under the
Normans. The adherents of the former theory are the stronger
in numbers and, during recent years, in authority as well, including not only Palgrave [4] and Kemble,[5] whose views are now
largely superseded, but also Schmid,[6] Vinogradoff,[7] Maitland,[8]
and above all Liebermann,[9] the latest and greatest specialist to

---

[1] *Plac. de Quo War.*, 303.

[2] *Ibid.* 93, 254, 456. Such a claim of the prior of Ely in Bergham by a grant
of St. Edward is, indeed, sustained (*ibid.* 729); but in this case the grant is
only in general terms, with no mention of view of frankpledge.

[3] As in Powell, *Antiquity of the Leet*, 8.

[4] *Commonwealth*, i. 202; ii. p. cxxiii.

[5] *Saxons in England*, i. 243–251.

[6] *Gesetze*, 646–648.

[7] *Growth of the Manor*, 198.

[8] Pollock and Maitland, *English Law* (1895), i. 558; Maitland, *Domesday
Book and Beyond*, 284.

[9] *Ueber die Leges Edw. Conf.*, 81, note 1.

investigate the subject. Yet the adoption of the Anglo-Norman theory by Gneist,[1] the able Marquardsen,[2] and the great constitutional historians Waitz[3] and Stubbs,[4] still gives good standing to the opposing school. The question as to the origin of frankpledge remains an open one. For the present, at least, an opinion must rest merely on a review of the facts concerning both Saxon and Norman peace suretyship which have been brought out in a half-century of discussion by some of the world's best scholarship.

In Anglo-Saxon England there were three different institutions which have at one time or another been regarded as bearing some relation to the early history of frankpledge. These were the *gegildan* or gild-brethren, the *teothing* or tithing (in the Latin of the records, *decenna*), and *borh* or suretyship (Latin, *plegium, fideiussio*). Information concerning all three is derived exclusively from the laws of the Anglo-Saxons, which, though formally enacted and recorded, give at best, like all other early Germanic codes, but a partial view of the legal system of the people. Of the three institutions, *borh* is the only one mentioned any considerable number of times. An understanding of the *gegildan* and the tithing can be had only by the piecing together of a very few meagre references.

The *gegildan*, who appear both in the laws of Ine[5] and in those of Alfred, were associates, one of whose objects, though probably not the only one, was the supplementing of the *maegth* bond by assumption of the legal obligation of the kindred whenever the family group was deficient. In the laws of Alfred it is provided that if a man have no paternal kinsmen his associates

---

[1] *English Constitution*, 152.
[2] *Haft und Bürgschaft*, 60 ff.
[3] *Verfassungsgeschichte*, i. 453.
[4] *Constitutional History*, i. 94–95.
[5] Chs. xvi, xxi, in Liebermann, *Gesetze*, i. 96, 98; Thorpe, *Laws*, i. 112, 116.

are to pay a third of his *wergeld*, and that if he lack maternal kinsmen also these *gegildan* are to pay half.[1] It is thus assumed that a man will have gild-brethren even though he have no relatives. The theory of Waitz, that these were only voluntary sureties,[2] has been refuted by the observation of Kemble, that the law was expressed in general terms and consequently not "directed to a particular and exceptional condition."[3] These *gegildan*, moreover, were not, as has been supposed, altogether "the associates of strangers and kinless people";[4] according to Ine's law,[5] as Gross has pointed out, they had relatives, apparently living in the same community with themselves.[6] Obviously a man whose paternal *maegth* was intact might need the aid of gildsmen in making good any deficiencies due to a failure of the maternal line, or vice versa. The institution has a demonstrable bearing on the origin of frankpledge only as showing an early tendency in West Saxon law to substitute for the mutual responsibility of the *maegth* a similar mutual responsibility of a non-kindred group. All authorities have long since rejected the old error of assuming that the association of the *gegildan* is identical with the frankpledge tithing;[7] but the student of primitive law still finds himself irresistibly drawn to the conclusion that, in the two centuries between Alfred and Henry I, when there is no mention of the *gegildan*, the legal principle of the old Saxon institution had considerable influence on frankpledge origins.[8]

---

[1] Alfred, xxvii, xxvii.1, in Liebermann, *Gesetze*, i. 66–67.

[2] *Verfassungsgeschichte*, i. 434.

[3] *Saxons in England*, i. 239.

[4] Stubbs, *Constitutional History*, i. 96, note 1.

[5] Ch. xxi, in Liebermann, *Gesetze*, i. 98–99.

[6] Gross, *Gild Merchant*, i. 177, note 2.

[7] Kemble, *Saxons in England*, i. 243.

[8] "A germ of the institution of compulsory frankpledge (*freeborgh*) may be seen in the voluntary association of the gegildan of Alfred's law, 27" (Vino-

The Anglo-Saxon tithing first appears in a local adaptation, for purposes of protection against theft, of the gild principle of mutual duty and mutual financial responsibility.   In the reign of Athelstan the bishops and reeves of the court of London ordained for the *frithgegildan* "eorlish and ceorlish" the set of regulations well known as the *Judicia Civitatis Lundoniae.*[1] According to these rules, Londoners were organized into groups of ten, each with a chief man to direct the other nine in the discharge of the duties set forth in the ordinance.[2]   The tens were in turn arranged in larger groups called *hyndens* or hundreds, the head man of each directing ten heads of tithings. These tithings were, however, far from being frankpledge groups; for their members did not act as sureties for each other. Their object was merely the capture and punishment of thieves, and the reimbursing of their own members for stolen property. Waitz has felicitously called such associations companies for insurance against cattle theft.[3]   As if to emphasize the difference between these tithings and those formed to afford suretyship for criminous members, the very ordinance directing the establishment of this London organization requires specifically a definite form of *borh* for a thief who is captured — preferably through his *maegth*,[4] but by pledge of others when the kinsmen

gradoff, *Growth of the Manor*, 277, note 78).   Konrad Maurer (in *Kritische Ueberschau*, i. 91) also believes that *frithborg* must have taken the place of *gegildan.*

[1] Liebermann, *Gesetze*, i. 173; Thorpe, *Laws*, i. 228. See also Liebermann, "Einleitung zum Statut der Londoner Friedensgilde unter Aethelstan," in *Mélanges Fitting*, ii. 79–103 (especially pp. 90–94, on the meaning of "Friedensgilde").

[2] *Judicia*, iii, in Liebermann, *Gesetze*, i. 175; Thorpe, *Laws*, i. 231.

[3] *Verfassungsgeschichte*, i. 434.

[4] 6 Athelstan, i. 4, xii. 2, in Liebermann, *Gesetze*, i. 174, 183. This is but a continuance of the *borh* system enforced by the three councils of Grateley, Exeter, and Thundersfield, in conformity with the mandates of which the London decree was enacted. See 6 Athelstan, Prol., *ibid.* 173. Cf. also 5 Athelstan, Prol., 3, and 4 Athelstan, ii, *ibid.* 166, 171.

will not serve. Further differences between the *frithgild* and
the frankpledge tithing are that the former was for *eorls* as well
as *ceorls*, the latter for the lower classes only, the former for
London alone,[1] the latter for the realm in general. The tithing
of this local experiment is thus a peculiar institution, entirely
different from the frankpledge tithing, and also quite distinct
from the ordinary Anglo-Saxon police tithing, which had no
gild feature.[2]

The police tithing makes its appearance in recorded legislation a little later than the London institution, which in the
absence of any definite information is thus naturally, though of
course with no degree of certainty, taken to be its prototype.[3]
Its head, the tithingman, is mentioned in the laws of Edgar
and Ethelred as a recognized peace official, a sort of under-
constable, who, like the head of the London ten of Athelstan's
reign, is directed by a hundredman.[4] The tithing itself as an
institution of the realm is expressly mentioned in the laws of
Canute some seventy years later, and every free man is then
required to be a member of one.[5] Liebermann's discovery
that in an Anglo-Saxon Bible of about the year 1000 the captain
of ten, the *decanus* of the Vulgate, is translated *teothingman*,[6]

---

[1] At about the same time a set of local enactments for Kent, without tithing
or *gegildan*, was decreed by a local *witan* for the purpose of carrying out the
same invocation of the king for the bettering of the peace of the realm in
accordance with which the London ordinance was made. See 3 Athelstan, v,
in Liebermann, *Gesetze*, i. 170.

[2] Konrad Maurer (in *Kritische Ueberschau*, i. 95) agrees with the generally
accepted idea that the London *frithgild* tithing and hundred have nothing in common with the tithing and hundred found elsewhere in the Anglo-Saxon kingdom.

[3] It is entirely possible that the London *frithgild* had modelled its tithing
and hundred on a regular territorial tithing and hundred of the realm.

[4] 1 Edgar, ii, iv (about A. D. 960), in Liebermann, *Gesetze*, i. 192–193;
Thorpe, *Laws*, i. 258. *Cf.* also "tungravius et decimales homines," 7 Ethelred,
ii. 5 (A. D. 992–1011), in Liebermann, i. 261.

[5] 2 Canute, xx, in Liebermann, i. 322–323; Thorpe, i. 386.

[6] Liebermann, *Ueber die Leges Edw. Conf.*, 80.

shows quite clearly that at the beginning of the eleventh century the head of the tithing was a well-known official of the realm, and that the tithing itself, which he led, was certainly known just as well. The two questions concerning this institution which have perplexed historians are whether it was a territorial or a personal division, and whether it had any connection with the origin of frankpledge.

The theory that the tithing was a fraction of the Anglo-Saxon hundred naturally presents itself; for not only does the word *teothing* mean a tenth,[1] but the head of the tithing was under the direction of the head of the hundred, and the London *frith-gild* tithing was actually a tenth of a hundred. From this suggested numerical relation many writers have undertaken to demonstrate a symmetrical development of Anglo-Saxon local institutions. The analogy of the German territorial hundred, as well as the undoubted territorial character of the English hundred at a little later period, incline the majority to believe that the hundred of the law of Edgar was a territorial division of the shire. If, then, the tithing be regarded as a tenth of a hundred, it can scarcely be held to be anything else than territorial,[2]

---

[1] The name is thus applied to the church tithe (see 2 Edgar, i. 1, in Liebermann, *Gesetze*, i. 196–197). The employment of tithingmen along with the town reeve and the priest to enforce alms and fasting vowed upon the sacred relics (7 Ethelred, ii. 5) shows how the ordinary police power in Anglo-Saxon days extended to ecclesiastical as well as to secular offences. Since the church tithe had been compulsory from the year 787 onward (Stubbs, *Constitutional History*, i. 248–250), it is not improbable that the tithingman was employed in the collection of it, and that the name by which he was called arose from this circumstance. Edgar carefully revised the regulations concerning the tithe; and the words "decimales homines" in the laws of Ethelred (above, p. 11, note 4) seem to point to an ecclesiastical origin of the name tithingman. If this interpretation is correct, the tithing of Anglo-Saxon law is clearly territorial, and is to be identified with the parish or township; furthermore, the thirteenth-century use of the word tithing as a synonym for the township of the old West Saxon kingdom can thus be easily explained.

[2] Marquardsen (*Haft*, 46) and Schmid (*Gesetze*, 648) hold that the tithing

although the language of the laws shows that membership in the tithing of Canute was a personal matter, just as membership in the court representing the hundred was personal. But, whatever the original nature of the tithing, it is clear enough that any system of policing based upon it must have approached, roughly at least, a territorial basis; for it was essential to the successful pursuit of a thief, not only that the tithing live in the neighborhood of the crime,[1] but that the members live near enough together for co-operation. The tithing which is found in the shires of the old West Saxon kingdom in the thirteenth century, and which at the present time exists nowhere in England except in these and sporadically in the adjacent shires,[2] was and is simply the local division elsewhere called the township;[3] and the tithingman was a township reeve who still had police and court duties by virtue of his position.[4] Nor can the theory that there were ten tithings in a hundred be lightly set aside; for even in

was purely territorial; but Gneist (*Verwaltungsrecht*, i. 51) believes that the hundred was territorial and the tithing a police division.

[1] Edgar's ordinance (1 Edgar, ii), which represents the initiative as coming from the hundredman, contemplates a situation under which it is necessary to call out more than one tithingman. The matter must first be made known to the hundredman; but it is hardly to be presumed that in ordinary cases pursuit was deferred until it could be authorized by a distant hundredman.

[2] Stubbs, *Constitutional History*, i. 92, note 2.

[3] To the possible objection that, if the tithing which was represented as common to the realm was territorial in the time of Canute, it should be found all over England to-day, there are two answers: (1) It is probable that the legislation of the West Saxon rulers was not strictly enforced in all parts of England; (2) The township may have been considered the equivalent of a tithing in the eleventh century just as well as in the thirteenth.

[4] Such a tithing was created in the thirteenth century by a decree requiring the ordinary township suit of court where it had not been enjoined before (*Calendar of Charter Rolls*, ii. 94). In the later period the tithingman frequently appears as the head of a frankpledge tithing; but it is by no means clear that this was always the case. The suit of court for the tithing was performed by the tithingman and four, just as that for the township was performed by the reeve and four. In Kent, where the tithing was called a *borgh*, such suit was by the *borhsealdor* and four. See below, p. 99.

the fourteenth century, after two hundred and fifty years of radical reorganization of English institutions, the number of tithings in a hundred in the former kingdom of Wessex was still in many cases near the number ten.[1]

The relation of the police tithing of Saxon England to the frankpledge tithing of Norman England must, then, be decided almost entirely on probability. The undeniably personal character of the police service rendered by the members of the Anglo-Saxon tithing at once suggests that, even if the tithing be regarded as a territorial institution, it nevertheless had some relation to the frankpledge group, which performed personal police service of a very similar nature. Moreover, the employment of a person at the head of the frankpledge tithing so nearly like the tithingman that twelfth-century writers assume the identity of the two, and the legal theory that the frankpledge group, like the London *frithgild* tithing of Athelstan, must consist of ten men, both indicate that, either directly or through tradition, the older tithing exercised a considerable influence upon the frankpledge group. Between the two there is, however, one fundamental difference, overlooked by older authorities, which at once precludes the idea that the tithing of the Anglo-Saxon laws is the original form of its namesake of frankpledge days. This difference lies in the fact that the former had nothing to do with suretyship, but was concerned only with the capture of criminals. The passage in the laws of Canute, of about 1030, requiring every free man above the age of twelve who wishes to be worthy of his *lad* and his *wer* to be in hundred and in tithing, and every one, whether hearth-fast or follower, to be in hundred and in surety (*borh*),[2] has sometimes been construed as showing that

---

[1] See *Feudal Aids*, vols. i–ii, *nomina villarum* in 1316 for Bucks, Dorset, Gloucester, and Hants.

[2] 2 Canute, xx, in Liebermann, *Gesetze*, i. 322–323; Thorpe, *Laws*, i. 386.

the tithing was a *borh* tithing; but the mere fact of the otherwise useless repetition proves the contrary.[1] The obvious truth is that at this time membership in a tithing did not provide a man with suretyship against breach of the peace; for, according to these same laws of Canute, the very classes of persons for whom a suretyship requirement was most necessary — those disobedient to summons, those suspected of crime, and those once convicted — had to find *borh* for themselves.[2] The contrary and erroneous view, held generally until within the last half-century, is due to the compiler of the so-called *Leges Henrici* (about 1115), who makes the first mention of frankpledge. His version of this law of Canute, made to suit the conditions of his own time, is that every one who wishes to be considered worthy of his *wer* and *wite* and free law shall be *in hundred and in tithing or frankpledge*, and that all freemen, both hearth-fast and retainers, shall be *in tithing*.[3] How the tithing could so have changed in the eighty-five years spanning the Norman Conquest that it was no longer recognized in its earlier form, is a matter which is to be explained only by the history of Saxon *borh* or suretyship.

The word *borh* (or *borg*, as it is sometimes written) was em-

---

[1] Ramsay's attempt (in his *Foundations of England*, i. 410) to prove that this is repetition depends on the statement of a twelfth-century writer who had been influenced by nearly a century of legal misconstruction of the passage to identify the tithing of Canute with the familiar frankpledge tithing of his day. So firm a believer in the Saxon origin of frankpledge as Liebermann (*Ueber die Leges Edw. Conf.*, 81) regards this passage as a proof that *borh* and tithing were still distinct. Marquardsen (*Haft*, 53) goes too far in assuming that the *heorthfest* and *folgere* were not free because under a lord's *borh*, and were therefore not the same class of persons as those in tithing.

[2] 2 Canute, xxx. 3*a–b*, xxxi, xxxiii, in Liebermann, *Gesetze*, i. 332–337 *passim*.

[3] *Leges Henrici*, viii. 1–2, *ibid.* 554. See the account of Stubbs (*Constitutional History*, i. 95), who, not having the advantage of Liebermann's dating of the *leges* of the twelfth century, supposed that it was the compiler of the *Leges Edward Confessoris* who first made this error.

ployed in Saxon England to designate suretyship in general.[1] It was used, for example, of the security given for the carrying out of a marriage contract,[2] of security for a debt, and consequently of the debt itself.[3] Even the assurance of the fulfilment of a promise made by calling upon God as a witness was called *Godborg*.[4] It was, however, with the use of *borh* as a means of securing justice of the criminal that the Saxon legislators of the tenth and eleventh centuries were chiefly concerned.

The origin of this latter form of suretyship is to be found in the responsibility of the *maegth*, or clan, for injuries committed by any of its members upon men of another clan. Such liability for paying the *wergeld* made clansmen in a sense sureties for each other. The state, as soon as it became strong enough to interfere in such matters, aided the injured in exacting reparation, and eventually came to stand itself in the light of a clan which held the kinsmen of wrongdoers responsible to the crown for rendering satisfaction for the crimes of their relatives. Thus, near the end of the seventh century occurs the earliest reference to *borh* for peace observance in the requirement of the Kentish laws of Hlothaere and Eadric that, if a man make complaint against another and cite him to appear either in the folk assembly or in a local court, the accused must give security to the complainant to do him justice as the Kentish magistrates prescribe.[5] In the same laws it is provided that a man who entertains at his house for more than three nights a stranger who comes over the mark shall, if any injury is done by his guest, be surety for him. After three nights the stranger becomes a member of the household and hence, in legal presumption, of

---

[1] Alfred, i. 8, in Liebermann, *Gesetze*, i. 48–49.

[2] Ine, xxxi, *ibid.* 102–103.

[3] Wright, *Vocabularies*, i. 21, 78, 115, 237, 358.

[4] Alfred, xxxiii, in Liebermann, *Gesetze*, i. 66–67.

[5] Hlothaere and Eadric, viii, *ibid.* 10; Thorpe, *Laws*, i. 30.

the family;[1] if he does any injury, therefore, the head of the household either must see that he appears in court and by a payment makes good the damage, or must himself make it good.

A few years later in the same century a similar modification of the collective responsibility of the kindred appears in West Saxon law. "If your *geneat* steals," says the law, "and escapes, if you have a pledge for him, remind him of the value of the stolen thing; if he has no pledge you pay."[2] The *borh* here is but one person, and possibly not of the offender's kindred; for the usual rules do not hold in the case of a man who is dependent upon a lord and perhaps of unfree status. According to a law of Edward the Elder, even the freeman with property, when accused of theft, was to be taken in *borh* by those who had commended him to his lord, that he might purge himself at the ordeal; or other friends might act in the same capacity. If the accused knew no one who would be pledge for his fulfilling his law, security might be taken of his property, and he might thus escape confinement pending judgment.[3] This near approach to modern bail was, however, not the rule when freemen had actually been convicted of crime; for even in the reign of Athelstan it was assumed that those who undertook responsibility for a man actually proved guilty by the ordeal were his relatives.[4] The state held a thief responsible in the amount of his *wergeld*,[5] and those who paid *wergeld* were the clansmen.

From this presumption that the *maegth* was ultimately respon-

---

[1] Hlothaere and Eadric, xv, in Liebermann, *Gesetze*, i. 11.

[2] Ine, xxii, *ibid*. 98–99.

[3] 2 Edward, iii, iii. 1, *ibid*. 142–143.

[4] 2 Athelstan, vi. 1, vii, *ibid*. 154–155. The man without land who served in another county was to be pledged by his relatives when he returned to visit them if they lodged him during the visit (2 Athelstan, viii, *ibid*.).

[5] 2 Athelstan, i. 1, *ibid*. 150–151.

2

sible for the deeds of one of its number arose a form of suretyship
for custody which served the purpose of the modern bond to keep
the peace. If through failure to find surety or *borh* an accused
person went to prison, he might on payment of a heavy fine be
released after a certain number of days upon condition that his
clansmen would consent to act as sureties for his future good
conduct.[1] If he repeated the crime of theft, they had either to
pay his *wergeld* or to return him to prison. This responsibility of the *maegth* as a guarantee of good behavior was also
employed in the case of men often accused of such crimes as
arson and witchcraft, as well as of those convicted at the ordeal.[2]

The general prevalence of commendation and of dependence
upon lords afforded a convenient means for the wider extension
of permanent suretyship. Before the middle of the tenth century such security was employed for men of the lower class who
had no lords, and who, because neither they nor their kindred
had standing in the community, could be brought to justice only
with difficulty.[3] The *maegth* of such a person was required to
find him a lord to insure his appearance. Surety to keep the
peace effected through the *maegth* thus tended, in a modified
form, to become surety to lead men to justice whenever they
were guilty of delinquency. In the reign of Athelstan is found
a Kentish regulation holding a lord responsible for pledging all
his men, — either directly, or, if there were many of them, indi-
rectly through a representative in each vill, — and empowering
him to require the relatives of a dependent to assume responsibility only when the reputation of the man was such that the
lord's reeve would not undertake the risk of standing pledge
for him. In such cases the discredited person had to find twelve

---

[1] 2 Athelstan, i. 3, in Liebermann, *Gesetze*, i. 150–151.
[2] 2 Athelstan, vi, vi. 1–2, *ibid.* 152–155 *passim.*
[3] 2 Athelstan, ii, *ibid.* 150–151.

of his kinsmen to act as pledges for him.[1] These relatives constituted a group somewhat similar to the frankpledge tithing, which will presently be observed more closely.

After Athelstan required that lordless men have standing suretyship the development of the *borh* system was rapid. In the next reign, that of Edmund, the lord was held responsible for making law-worthy whatever men were on his lands, and the officers were also required to bring under pledge all men oft accused and all of ill report.[2] Finally, about 960, in a law of Edgar appeared the last step in the establishment of general peace suretyship. Every man was now to see that he had a pledge to lead him to the fulfilment of justice in all cases; and this pledge, if the principal fled, was bound to stand in his place and bear what the criminal ought to bear.[3] Such was the unique plan for enforcing law that was followed for the century preceding the end of Saxon rule; but, as subsequent enactments show, it included only the freemen of the realm of the poorer, or non-noble, class,[4] and it did not compel members of a lord's household establishment whom he lodged to seek for surety, the lord being required to have them in his own *borh*.[5]

The *borh* pledge was constituted in two ways: according to the law of Edgar an ordinary person needed only one surety, but for the man of bad reputation there must be several.[6] The first method declined for a time in scope, and then remained stationary as long as English law required peace suretyship; it is the development of the second that throws light on the origin of frankpledge.

---

[1] 3 Athelstan, vii, vii. 1–2, in Liebermann, *Gesetze*, 170.

[2] 3 Edmund, vii, vii. 1, from *Quadripartitus*, *ibid*. 191.

[3] 3 Edgar, vi, vi. 1, *ibid*. 202–203.

[4] 1 Ethelred, Prol., and i, i. 8, 9*a*, 10, 12, 13; 2 Canute, xx, xx*a*: *ibid*. 216–219, 322–323.

[5] 1 Ethelred, i. 10; 2 Canute, xxxi: *ibid*. 218–219, 334–335.

[6] 3 Edgar, vi. 2, vii, *ibid*. 202–205.

When one person served as *borh* it seems always to have been
the lord who assumed the old responsibility of the *maegth*. It
has been observed that in Athelstan's time the Kentish lord, or
his reeve for him, had to act as *borh* against theft for all his
dependents in his vills except such as were of bad reputation,
a class still pledged by their kindred. The law of Edmund
made the lord surety for all who were on his lands and in his
peace. From the time of Athelstan, persons without property
who were likely to become criminals were required to be under
lordship, that they might the more easily be brought to account.
In the reigns of Edgar and Ethelred it was regularly taken for
granted that an oft-accused, or *tyhtbysig*, man would have a
lord, who was so far responsible for him that he had to be recom-
pensed in case the person fled under accusation,[1] but who may
have put the burden of obligation for such a dependent upon his
reeve.[2] In the reigns of Edmund, Ethelred, and Canute, special
legislation made the lord *borh* for the members of his own household, his *hiredmen*, whose *wergeld* he had to pay to the king if
any of them were not produced for judgment when accused.[3]
Legal writers of the twelfth and thirteenth centuries show that
the lord or the man of rank presented to justice only his household or mainpast. This small part of the population was thus
never brought under reciprocal suretyship, and hence is removed
from any connection with the formation of a real frankpledge
system. The greater number were, however, gradually drawn
to collective pledging.

The Anglo-Saxon custom of presenting an offender to justice
through a *borh* group of several persons is mentioned only when
such an offender is either a *tyhtbysig* man or a man once con-

---

[1] 3 Edgar, vii. 1; 1 Ethelred, i. 7: Liebermann, *Gesetze*, i. 204-205, 218-219.
[2] See above, p. 18.
[3] 3 Edmund, iii; 1 Ethelred, i. 10-11; 2 Canute, xxxi, xxxi*a*, xxxi.1: *ibid.*
190, 218-219, 334-335.

victed of crime. In the reign of Athelstan it was assumed that these sureties would be the criminal's kinsmen. Twelve, it has been said, was the number of the *maegth* required to act as surety for a Kentish man of untrustworthy character. Athelstan's laws show that, if a man had been accused or convicted once, his *maegth* were regularly expected to stand *borh* for him against a second offence,[1] a circumstance that proves the existence of group surety for certain contingencies in parts of England other than Kent. Moreover, the Kentish *maegth* group of twelve for surety purposes had strong affinity with certain other *maegth* groups in England. It seems, for example, more than a coincidence that its number was exactly the same as that of the *werborh*, whom, according to the law of Edmund, the slayer of a man had to find among his relatives to stand surety for the payment of the dead man's *wer* to the injured *maegth*.[2] Again, according to a law which Liebermann considers as belonging somewhere between 944 and 1060, and which no doubt follows an ancient clan custom, the *werborg* in case of the killing either of a *twelfhynd* or of a *twyhynd* man consisted of twelve men.[3] Even in the twelfth century, as the late Miss Bateson has shown, compurgators were in London and some other English boroughs

---

[1] 2 Athelstan, i. 3–4, vi.1, vii, in Liebermann, *Gesetze*, i. 150–155 *passim*.

[2] 2 Edmund, vii, vii. 1–2, *ibid.* 188–191.

[3] *Wergeldzahlung*, iii, vii, *ibid.* 392–395 *passim*. Eight were to be from the *maegth* of the slayer's father, four from the *maegth* of his mother. The *Leges Edw. Conf.*, xxxvi. 1 (*ibid.* 666), say twelve from the father's *maegth* and six from the mother's; but this is a late and less reliable authority. A provision in the regulations for the Northumberland priests, of a date within forty years prior to the Norman Conquest, seems to show an ecclesiastical modification of this usage in requiring that each priest shall find twelve pledges for his observance of the regulations. A breaking of them usually entailed a fine of twelve *ore*, which was also the amount of the *manbote* of the *sokeman* and *villanus* in the Danelaw. See *Leges Edw. Conf.*, xii. 4, *ibid.* 638.

twelve in number, and were required to be kinsmen of the principal; and in London the number of *borh* pledges enjoined was also twelve. It is reasonable, therefore, to accept her suggestion that the twelve kinsmen who served as sureties and compurgators are to be connected with the origin of the frankpledge group, the unit which succeeded to the responsibility of the *maegthborh*.[1] That such group suretyship may be traced to within about three decades of the year 1066 is shown by the law of Edmund requiring the reeve and the thegn, under heavy penalties, to put in *borh* the oft-accused man and the man of ill report,[2] by the repetition in the laws of Ethelred and Canute of enactments to enforce this duty,[3] and by the requirement, repeated in the laws of both the last-named kings, that the man who failed at the ordeal must have trustworthy sureties (*borgas*) against future misconduct.[4] The persistence of the responsibility of the kindred, therefore, indicates that the principle of *borh* through a group of twelve continued in force as late as the Norman Conquest at least.

A process by which collective *borh* became more and more prevalent during the last century of Anglo-Saxon rule, while the *borh* of the lord was employed less and less frequently, is reasonably clear, though it is not a matter of record. All freemen had to be in *borh*, and there were apparently only the two forms. It was in the interest of the lord to have the collective form employed whenever possible; for, when the man of doubtful reputation was disavowed and put under the suretyship of his kinsmen, the lord was freed from a grievous responsibility. Moreover, when there was any question as to a defendant's

---

[1] Bateson, *Borough Customs* (Selden Soc.), ii. pp. xxiv, xxviii.

[2] 3 Edmund, vii. 2, in Liebermann, *Gesetze*, i. 191.

[3] 1 Ethelred, iv. iv. 1; 2 Canute, xxxiii. xxxiii. 1: *ibid.* 220–221, 336–337.

[4] 1 Ethelred, i. 5; 2 Canute, xxx. 3*a*–*b*: *ibid.* 218–219, 332–333.

standing, the lord could not have been slow to take advantage of a doubt that would clear himself of liability. Furthermore, it is quite certain that for a long time before the Norman Conquest some lords held justiciary rights which gave them a special means of regulating the *borh* of their dependents through the control of a hundred court,[1] the agency that maintained the *borh* system. Maitland holds that, according to the old law requiring any one who had an accusation against a lord's dependent to seek justice first of the lord,[2] the latter had the option either of producing the offender in court, or of settling the demand of the accuser and exacting from the defendant both the amount of the claim and a *wite* for himself.[3] Such a scheme would naturally incline the lord to look sharply to the maintenance of group suretyship for all those likely to be accused, that he might at least have a means of producing them when required, but particularly that he might be assured of the payment of the *wite* which he gained by settling the matter himself.[4] When in addition to these seigniorial influences, which Maitland regards as sufficient to explain the origin of frankpledge,[5] it is considered that the *borh* of a group of neighbors or kinsmen was far more effective both as a deterrent from crime and as a means of apprehension than that of the lord could possibly be,[6] it need occasion no surprise to find that by the twelfth century the responsibility of the lord was limited to the members of his

---

[1] Maitland, *Domesday Book and Beyond*, 260–290, especially 260, 268–269.

[2] Athelstan's Grateley Law, 2 Athelstan, iii, in Liebermann, *Gesetze*, i. 152–153.

[3] Maitland, *Domesday Book and Beyond*, 284.

[4] This principle is a development based on two centuries of experience with the law of Ine: "If your *geneat* steals and escapes, if you have a pledge for him, remind him of the value of the stolen thing; if he has no pledge you pay." See above, p. 17.

[5] *Domesday Book and Beyond*, 284.

[6] It is this feature of collective responsibility in criminal matters that explains the popularity and rapid rise of the police tithing.

immediate household, while all others were under collective suretyship.

A striking change that seems to have come over the *borh* group between 950 and 1115 is the loss of its *maegth* character, a change that was in keeping with the decline of the *maegth* in all directions during the same period and with the corresponding increase in the power of the state. Though this change is never specifically mentioned in the law codes, a hint of it is to be found in the fact that, whereas in the laws of Athelstan collective suretyship always appears as *maegth* suretyship, in the laws of Ethelred and Canute there is merely the general requirement of sureties, with nothing to indicate that such vouchers were expected to be of the offender's kindred. Besides this inevitable tendency toward a change that set in as society gained the conception of a higher principle of organization than through the clan, the influence of lordship and the severity of the criminal law were factors bringing the *borh* group away from a *maegth* basis. The personal service of a man to his lord was, indeed, one of the most potent impulses in weakening the old *maegth* bond and in preparing the way for a new European society, especially since, with the growth of lordship, there came a corresponding increase of group pledging as a means of decreasing the lord's personal responsibility for his dependents. No one can conceive of a lord's making it obligatory that the twelve who took off his hands the responsibility for an unruly dependent should uniformly be of the man's *maegth;* for at times it was clearly impossible to find that number, and, even when possible, it was in many cases not the easiest means of effecting what the lord desired. Furthermore, in the reigns of Ethelred and Canute the man of bad reputation, for whom the lord would under no condition be accountable even half a century earlier, was compelled either by the reeve or by the posse from the hundred court to find *borh* under penalty of forfeiting his life and filling a felon's grave.[1] Such a law admits of little stickling on the point that a man's sureties be his relatives. In the failure of the *maegth*, in its refusal to serve, or in the decline of its old responsibility, it must have been practically impossible that any sufficient person, who through pity or friendship would assume part of the obligation to save life, should not be an acceptable surety. In the Danelaw, moreover, — that part of England where personal lordship seems to have been least frequent, and where the frankpledge group of a later age was apparently most independent of the territorial unit, — there was no *maegth* organization,[2] a circumstance from which it may be regarded as certain that collective suretyship for most of the men was effected here simply through a number of neighbors. By Canute's time the same plan must also have been followed to a large extent in other parts of England.[3]

Reviewing the available information concerning Anglo-Saxon *borh* down to the enactment of the laws of Canute, one finds that a comparison of that institution with frankpledge reveals striking similarities, but no less striking contrasts. Both systems were of vast importance in securing peace observance among the lower classes, each being in its day, to borrow Green's expression, "the base of social order."[4] In each was apparent a conscious direction by a general authority

---

[1] 1 Ethelred, iv, iv. 1; 2 Canute, xxxiii, xxxiii. 1: Liebermann, *Gesetze*, i. 220–221, 336–337.

[2] This the writer has upon the authority of Professor Vinogradoff.

[3] Green (*Conquest of England*, 229) is thus right in supposing that the *borh* of this period was founded on the "free engagement of neighbour for neighbour"; but he errs in assuming that it was frankpledge. Kemble (*Saxons in England*, i. 251–252) suggests that such a system in the hands of the neighborhood had an advantage over one founded upon kinship, in that it obviated an improper partiality to some of the members, a tendency inherent in the bond of blood.

[4] *Conquest of England*, 229.

in painstaking legislation and administrative regulation, a fact
which clearly shows that, in spite of all the acquisition of jurisdictional power and influence by lords, the hand in control was
that of the central government. The local supervision of
Saxon *borh* and Norman frankpledge rested with the same
tribunal, the hundred court,[1] which probably held two sessions
a year chiefly for the purpose of administering the detail of the
earlier plan, just as it held two for the execution of the later
one.[2] Excluding from Saxon *borh* the class pledged by lords
(a class never in frankpledge proper but still found in the frankpledge age), each system put under suretyship all the rest of
the men of the realm who were of non-noble status,[3] and each
put them under collective suretyship. Finally, the *borh* system
was in all probability not maintained throughout the kingdom,
just as frankpledge certainly was not; and the regions without
frankpledge seem also to have been without *borh*.[4] These two
institutions, therefore, possess such strong points of identity in
purpose, method, and territory occupied that their maintenance
at one and the same time would have been not only an absurdity
but an impossibility. Had frankpledge existed in England
prior to 1030, the Saxon *borh* system, devised and maintained
with infinite pains, would have been a superfluity.[5] The Anglo-

---

[1] See 3 Edgar, vii. 1; and 2 Canute, xxv, xxv*a*, xxv. 2: Liebermann, *Gesetze*,
i. 204–205, 328–329.

[2] See below, pp. 115–116.

[3] The Anglo-Saxon legal principle that the lord was ultimately responsible
for the dependent provided for those of unfree status. Hence, remembering
that the *leges* of the twelfth century still regarded the villains as free, one may
say that *borh* included all freemen, whether pledged by the lord or by neighbors or relatives, and that frankpledge included all freemen not pledged by
the lord. Compare 3 Edgar, vi; 1 Ethelred, i; 2 Canute, xx *a* (Liebermann, i.
202–203, 216–217, 322–323), with *Leges Henrici*, viii. 2, and *Leges Edw. Conf.*,
xx (*ibid.* 554, 645).

[4] See below, pp. 52–53, 56–58.

[5] This argument of Marquardsen (*Haft*, 25, 45) shows how illogical is the
old practice of reading *friborg* where *borg* occurs in the Saxon laws.

Norman scheme of peace suretyship was clearly the offspring and successor of the Anglo-Saxon institution.

The contrasts between *borh* and frankpledge are those between a less highly and a more highly developed system. The *borh* obligation of the laws of Ethelred and Canute was not permanent, as was that of frankpledge suretyship. It was voluntary, its assumption for a person of bad reputation was optional,[1] and apparently it might be withdrawn so long as no legal imposition thereby incurred remained undischarged. The pledges of a convicted person were, indeed, permitted to withdraw; for the law required such a person to give new ones,[2] a point in marked contrast to the compulsory obligation of those in frankpledge. According to the Anglo-Saxon laws, furthermore, every man had his individual *borh* independent of that of other men. He need not — when his surety was his lord, he could not — render compensatory service as *borh* for those who pledged him. Under the frankpledge system, on the other hand, the pledges all belonged to a fixed group and served as reciprocal sureties.[3] Finally, the frankpledge group was not, like the Anglo-Saxon *borh* group, merely an association to effect suretyship; it was also a tithing, a body of ten members performing police duties under the direction of a head man. To sum up the case, all that the collective *borh* of Canute's reign required in order to become frankpledge was that its suretyship obligation be assumed by the tithing or a similar group, and that it be made compulsory upon the group.

The fusion of *borh* and tithing, which were regarded as legally distinct about the year 1030,[4] was easily accomplished in actual

---

[1] As Ramsay (*Foundations of England*, i. 378) well shows.

[2] See above, p. 22.

[3] This is emphasized by Waitz (*Verfassungsgeschichte*, i. 446–447) and by Liebermann (*Ueber die Leges Edw. Conf.*, 81).

[4] It was Liebermann who pointed out (*ibid.*) that this was the process by which frankpledge originated.

practice, no doubt in many cases by this very date. This is probably the reason why in the old law the two systems appear in such juxtaposition as to have given rise to the erroneous notion of their identity.[1] According to the same legislation, all persons are through the hundred court to be brought into tithings and all are to be in suretyship. The members of the tithing to which all the freemen of a given neighborhood belong are the same persons who must unite to form *borh* associations for each other in the ever-increasing number of instances in which neither the lord nor the relatives act as sureties. Old Anglo-Saxon legal tradition indicates that the two forms of organization included very nearly the same number of persons, — the tithing ten, the *maegthborh* twelve, — figures that may be taken to stand approximately for the number of men in a small village. Both groups, consisting to a greater or a less degree of the same persons, joined in the pursuit of criminals, the tithing to fulfil its regular duties, the *borh* to capture the criminal whom they had pledged and thus to escape a heavy payment;[2] and both were held to their duties through enrolment in the same hundred court. Under the influence of this contact year by year, the voluntary and occasional *borh* group became assimilated with the compulsory and regular tithing group. At the first mention of frankpledge, eighty-five years after the laws of Canute were enacted, the suretyship unit consisted not of

---

[1] "And we will that every freeman, be he householder, be he follower, be brought into a hundred and into tithing, who desires his *lad* and *wer* and free law in case any one should slay him after he have reached the age of xii years. And let every one be brought into a hundred and in *borh* and let the *borh* hold and lead him to every plea." — 2 Canute, xx, xx*a*, in Liebermann, *Gesetze*, i. 322–323.

[2] Two hundred shillings, the *wergeld* of the ordinary freeman, was a heavy financial burden. In the reign of Athelstan a good horse was valued at a half-pound, an ox at a mancus, a cow at twenty pence, a swine at ten pence, and a sheep at a shilling. See *Judicia Civitatis Lundoniae*, vi. 1–2, *ibid.* 176.

twelve men, the *borh* number, but of ten, the tithing number. So complete was the amalgamation, at least in matters touching suretyship, that in the twelfth and thirteenth centuries the only surviving monument to the former separation of the two institutions was apparently the formularistic legal expression "in tithing and in *friborg*," [1] though it is possible that the troublesome name *douzaine* or dozen, which is applied to the tithing in the law French of the thirteenth century,[2] may be a relic of the same Anglo-Saxon condition. The clearest indication of the amalgamation itself is to be found in the extreme southeast of England, where by the twelfth century the local division of the hundred was often called, not a township or a tithing, but a *borg*.[3]

The final step in the evolution of frankpledge, the legal identification of the collective suretyship obligation with the tithing, is a development which, though promoted by the actual practice just described, was nevertheless perfected by further means. At this point ends the Anglo-Saxon growth of the system under discussion. The tithing and the *borh* are old English institutions; the rise of neighborhood collective suretyship through the decline of seigniorial and kinship pledging, and even the blending of the tithing and collective suretyship in practical operation, both belong to the period before 1066. Between the voluntary pledging of a man by his neighbors in 1030, however, and the duty, in 1115, of every man in a tithing to serve as a surety for every other man in the tithing without right of refusal or withdrawal, no matter what the character of

---

[1] "Sine plegio et tedingam" (1180), Madox, *Firma Burgi*, 64, note *e;* "in no tithing nor in frankpledge" (12 Hen. III), Salt Archaeol. Soc., *Collections*, iv. 72; "habeant inter se tethingam et frithborg," *Cart. St. Peter of Gloucester* (Rolls Series), ii. 36; "in franco plegio et decenna," Bracton, fol. 124*b*, ii. 304.

[2] See below, p. 87.

[3] See below, p. 86.

the associates, is a break that can be explained only by governmental action of a deliberate and rigorous nature prompted by
the imminent danger to which the public peace was exposed
from the ordinary freemen of the realm.[1]   In vain does one look
for this causal condition during the reigns of the sons of Canute
or in that of Edward the Confessor. Theirs was a quiet period
for the realm in general; for, as Liebermann points out,[2] the
hatred against Edward's Norman favorites led to the hostile
intrigues of great nobles at court rather than to violence from
the people in the country districts. The dispersion throughout
England of a considerable number of foreign conquerors,
whether after the conquest by the Danish Canute or after that
by the Norman William, explains the situation exactly. But
Canute made no decided change in the English *borh* system;
he even sent home his foreign troops,[3] protecting his followers
while in England only by re-enacting the law of Ethelred under
which the king was declared *maegth* and *mundbora* of strangers,
with the duty of avenging their injuries.[4] William the Conqueror, however, in a drastic regulation for the avowed protection of his followers from assassination, — a mandate by which
he held the whole hundred accountable,[5] — laid bare a condition

---

[1] Vinogradoff (*Growth of the Manor*, 250, note 36) merely says that frankpledge "sprang up naturally when the system of *maegborh* had spent itself."
Maitland (*Domesday Book and Beyond*, 284) suggests nothing more than that
the influence of the lord in the growth of collective suretyship accounts for
frankpledge.   Liebermann (*Ueber die Leges Edw. Conf.*, 81) attributes its
origin to a blending of *borh* and tithing before the twelfth century, preferably between 1030 and 1086.   No one has ever given a more logical statement of the
final influence in the organization of frankpledge than Waitz (*Verfassungsgeschichte*, i. 453), who declares for "the strong police power, probably that
of William I."

[2] *Ueber die Leges Edw. Conf.*, 113.

[3] Stubbs, *Select Charters*, 75.

[4] 8 Ethelred, xxxiii; 2 Canute, xl: Liebermann, *Gesetze*, i. 267, 340–341.
Palgrave (*Commonwealth*, i. 196) attributes the origin of frankpledge to Canute.

[5] See Liebermann, *Ueber die Leges Edw. Conf.*, 112–113.

and a motive to warrant a more stringent *borh* system. The need of strong measures to secure the observance of peace by the peasants, the marked change that came over the suretyship system betokening a strong organizing hand which was not at the helm before 1066, the similarity of the new mutual and compulsory responsibility of the tithing to that of the hundred known to have been introduced by William, the fact that comparatively early in the reign of his son Henry I the frankpledge tithing appears to have been a well-established institution customary even in past time,[1] as well as the facts that about thirty years after his death the process of putting men in frankpledge tithings was uniform and well known,[2] and that by 1125 a native writer was completely in ignorance as to the origin of the system,[3] all point to the reign of William the Conqueror, from 1066 to 1087, as the period of legal organization.

The Normans in England did not, then, create an out-and-out new system of suretyship; as Bishop Stubbs clearly shows, they merely adapted an old English system to the needs of their own time.[4] Frankpledge was probably unknown in Normandy and unfamiliar to the experience of the new kings. Its name seems to be nothing but a Norman version of the word used in the everyday speech of the English people; and for its characteristic official, the tithingman, a name familiar in English law a century before the Norman Conquest, no French word is used

---

[1] Note the word *debebant* in *Leges Edw. Conf.*, xx. 1 (Liebermann, *Gesetze*, i. 645). See also below, p. 60, note 1.

[2] *Leges Henrici*, viii. 2, *ibid.* 554 (1114–1118).

[3] See above, p. 6.

[4] "The institution of the collective Frankpledge, which recent writers incline to treat as a Norman innovation, is so distinctly coloured by English custom that it has been generally regarded as purely indigenous. If it were indeed a precaution taken by the new rulers against the avoidance of justice by the absconding or harbouring of criminals, it fell with ease into the usages and even the legal terms which had been common for other similar purposes since the reign of Athelstan." — Stubbs, *Constitutional History*, i. 299.

by the earlier writers.[1] Moreover, William's legal position was that of an English king. As such he accepted the constitution of Edward the Confessor and the laws of the English people, except in the few instances in which he specifically modified them. One of the few *leges* which are generally regarded as embodying genuine legislation of his directs that the hundred be held as in the time of Edward the Confessor, and repeats the old law that every freeman must have surety to lead him to justice,[2] the only noteworthy innovation being a provision which shows that pledges are usually required to clear themselves from collusion in the escape of a criminal. Last of all, the absence of frankpledge from those parts of England where it is least probable that the Anglo-Saxon *borh* laws were enforced — Yorkshire in particular[3] — shows that the Norman frankpledge was merely an adaptation of the older system, not a creation for the Conqueror's new domain.

The arguments against the initiation of the real frankpledge system through Norman reorganization furthered by processes already far advanced before they had formal legal recognition, are not convincing. Since the advocates of an Anglo-Saxon origin have gone no farther than to demonstrate an undeniable development from old English institutions, and to discredit the idea of a Norman creation, the balance of probability still inclines strongly away from the view that frankpledge as already

---

[1] The ordinary French term *chef plege*, or capital pledge, a word having to do solely with the Norman suretyship system, was, however, probably in legal use before 1135, as is indicated by the words "in omni friborge unus erat capitalis, quem ipsi [*i. e.* Angli] vocabant friborges heved" (*Leges Edw. Conf.*, xx. 3, in Liebermann, *Gesetze*, i. 646).

[2] *Willelmi I Articuli X*, viii, viiia (also French *Articuli*, viii, viiia), *ibid.* 488–489. See also Stubbs, *Select Charters*, 84. In the form handed down to modern times the law shows a relaxed rather than an increased severity in excusing the pledges from paying the *wergeld* of the fugitive if they can clear themselves of complicity in his crime.

[3] See below, pp. 49–55.

described came into being before 1066 unaided by the legal genius apparent in the strongly centralized Norman governmental system. The scholarship of Liebermann designates the end of the Conqueror's reign as the earliest point to which the complete blending of *borh* and tithing may with probability be assigned.[1] His suggestion that the silence of Domesday is very striking if frankpledge was founded within the preceding twenty years has little force as argument; for Domesday, being a financial survey, is not necessarily concerned with the kind of suretyship required. This very silence, indeed, and the persistence of the English name *friborg*, also advanced by Liebermann as evidence of Anglo-Saxon origin,[2] accord well with William's policy of nominally retaining old English institutions while actually modifying them — in spirit, at least — as occasions and conditions demanded. It was in the Norman interest to encourage the idea that the compulsory, mutual pledging of the tithing was the same as that system of free pledging under which the members of the local tithing had undertaken to act as sureties for each other; and the populace was not likely to change the old name merely because common practice had become legal requirement.

Of greater significance, though by no means conclusive as proof, is the fact that writers of the twelfth century who first mention frankpledge believed it to be an Anglo-Saxon institution. This line of argument, first advanced by Schmid chiefly to show that frankpledge could not have originated in the reign of William II or of Henry I, during the lifetime of these writers,[3] loses much of its force when applied to the earlier reign of William I. Liebermann attaches importance to the fact that the idea of an Anglo-Saxon origin was held in common by Wil-

---

[1] *Ueber die Leges Edw. Conf.*, 81.
[2] *Ibid.*, note 1.
[3] Schmid, *Gesetze*, 647, with reference to the *Gesta Regum* (Rolls Series), i. 129–130.

3

liam of Malmesbury and the writer of the *Leges Edwardi Confessoris;* [1] and one may note that the same idea was entertained by the compiler of the *Leges Henrici*, as is shown by his interpreting frankpledge into the laws of Canute.[2] These ancient writers, however, make grave errors concerning the system which considerably impair their value as authorities. So far as they express any idea, they believe that the institution was suddenly created; [3] and they all hold the erroneous notion that it existed in every part of England.[4] Furthermore, that they are not reliable witnesses concerning important institutional changes in the reign of William the Conqueror is shown by the fact that, according to the compiler of the *Leges Edwardi*, the fine undoubtedly first laid upon the hundred by William for failure to produce the murderer of a person whose English descent could not be proved [5] was instituted by Canute,[6] according to William of Malmesbury by Alfred.[7] The truth is that neither of these writers had knowledge of the Conqueror's reign at first hand.[8] The legend of Alfred's legal innovations, and the mention of a

[1] *Ueber die Leges Edw. Conf.*, 78; 81, note 1.

[2] See above, p. 15.

[3] See above, p. 6.

[4] Liebermann himself points out these facts in his *Ueber die Leges Edw. Conf.*, 79.

[5] *Ibid.* 112–113. There are still extant versions, older than 1135, of what purports to be William's decree introducing the murder fine. See *Leis Willelme*, xxii, in Liebermann, *Gesetze*, i. 510–511; and *Willelmi I Articuli X*, iii. 1–2, *ibid.* 487.

[6] *Leges Edw. Conf.*, xvi, *ibid.* 642; Thorpe, *Laws*, i. 449; Schmid, *Gesetze*, 500.

[7] *Gesta Regum* (Rolls Series), i. 129–130.

[8] William was not born before 1095 (*ibid.*, Introd., p. xiv). The compiler of the *Leges Edwardi*, which, according to Liebermann, were probably written between 1135 and 1150, could hardly have been born much earlier; but if 1115, the earliest possible date for them, be accepted, it is still to be remembered that the writer was a foreigner (Liebermann, *Ueber die Leges Edw. Conf.*, 17–18), who could not have been conversant with English affairs until about 1095.

tithing — supposedly a frankpledge tithing — in old English laws, sufficiently account for their notion that frankpledge was maintained before the Norman Conquest. Their ignorance in regard to an important system clearly organized by William I shows that their failure to understand and explain a Norman adaptation of an old English institution is of slight importance as argument. More than this, there is a perfectly clear reason why foreign-born writers should, at least in the reign of Henry I, have been influenced, as the compiler of the *Leges Henrici* certainly was influenced,[1] by an inclination to further the king's desire for popularity with his English subjects by representing his administrative practices as resting, not on innovations of Norman oppression, but on the good old laws of Edward the Confessor.[2]

The reorganization of the English *borh* system at the hands of the Norman government, effected somewhere between 1066 and about 1100, was prompted by the rebellious and murderous attitude of the vanquished Anglo-Saxons toward their conquerors. In old English law the man of bad reputation was expected to be under collective suretyship because no lord was willing to risk responsibility for him. In the Norman period it was the local uprisings following the Conquest, together with a state of the peace under which the king found it necessary to take drastic steps to protect Normans from secret assassination, that led the new foreign lords to refuse the responsibility of pledging English dependents outside of their own households. Except in case of the comparatively small class of household retainers, the option of finding one sufficient person to stand as *borh*, allowed in the time of Canute and apparently till 1066, now disappears.

---

[1] He was a lawyer associated with the *curia regis*. See Davis, in *Eng. Hist. Review*, xvii. 148.

[2] Liebermann (*Ueber die Leges*, etc., 78, 112) suggests this influence.

The *borh* law, commonly regarded as one of the real enactments of William the Conqueror and dating in a written form
from the reign of Henry I, makes a marked legal innovation in
assuming that every man, not merely the *tyhtbysig* one, will have
a number of pledges.[1] The whole English people, classed like
its own malefactors of an earlier time, was thus required to be
in collective suretyship. "All villains," says the oldest version
of the so-called laws of William [2] (that is to say, all the ordinary
men of the vills),[3] "shall be in frankpledge."

The withdrawal of the right to find one's own pledges and
thus to have an individual suretyship group was a necessary
part of the repressive movement by which William the Conqueror brought out of lawlessness a famous observance of the
public peace.[4] This achievement was effected largely through
the introduction of a principle new to English law, — that of
communal responsibility in criminal matters, a principle applied
to the township and the tithing as well as to the hundred. In
its earliest form it seems to appear in the heavy fine laid upon
a hundred which failed to produce the murderer of one of
William's followers. After this to put the lesser divisions of the
hundred under the same sort of bond was an easy step, which
brought nearer home to each locality its obligation to preserve
the peace. It is a significant fact that the responsibility of four
neighboring vills in criminal affairs, a circumstance very famil-

---

[1] "Si quisquam talium evaserit, videant plegii ut simpliciter solvant quod
calumniatum est, et purgent se." — *Willelmi I Articuli X*, viiia, in Liebermann, *Gesetze*, i. 488.

[2] The French translation (*Leis Willelme*, xx. 3a, *ibid.* 506), dating from the
reign of Henry I.

[3] See Maitland, *Domesday Book and Beyond*, 37, 43, 51–52.

[4] "Among other things is not to be forgotten the good peace that he made
in this land; so that a man who had any confidence in himself might go over
his realm, with his bosom full of gold, unhurt. Nor durst any man slay
another man had he done ever so great evil to the other." — *Anglo-Saxon
Chronicle* (Rolls Series), ii. 189.

iar to Englishmen of the twelfth and thirteenth centuries, is not found in English law before the Conquest. In the thirteenth century there are numerous recorded instances in which vills and even boroughs were accounted hundreds in the exaction of the *murdrum;*[1] and even in the *leges* of the twelfth century such an obligation of a small community has considerable sanction.[2] It was inevitable that suretyship regulations should fall into this scheme of local responsibility. Now that the government had to guard carefully against the complicity of sureties in the crime and flight of their pledges,[3] the best way, both to prevent their running away together and to collect fines in case of flight, was to make every man in the community responsible for every other man. To accomplish this result, the simple device, employed by Norman officials, of collecting the fine from the community at large when it failed to produce an absconding miscreant was, as Gneist shows, sufficient; but to make this practice, as Gneist does, the one explanation of the origin of frankpledge is to ignore a century and a half of Anglo-Saxon legal history.[4] The former

[1] As in Madox, *Firma Burgi*, 85, note *x;* Madox, *Exchequer*, 544.

[2] Liebermann, *Ueber die Leges Edw. Conf.*, 109. According to *Leges Henrici*, xci. 2–3, the *manerium* pays; one translation of *Leis Willelme*, xxii, says the *homines de visineto*. See Liebermann, *Gesetze*, i. 511, 607.

[3] See *Willelmi I Articuli X*, viii, viiia, *ibid.* 488.

[4] "The Norman official," says Gneist (*English Constitution*, 152), "who had nothing in common with the communities, summarily demanded the fine from the people *tributim* (in gross), and left them to settle the matter among themselves. The result was that in this manner the system of police sureties developed into a mutual responsibility of the tithing." His idea that the change was from one or two pledges only to the pledging of the whole community does not accord with facts already brought out in connection with *maegthborh*. It must be borne in mind, too, that the responsibility of the vill or the tithing was not merely that of the hundred applied to a smaller district; for the hundred was held accountable only when it failed to produce the slayer of a person whose English ancestry could not be proved, the frankpledge tithing whenever one of its members escaped after committing any felony. Thus the old Anglo-Saxon suretyship duties were retained. Both Stubbs (*Constitutional History*, i. 95) and Liebermann (*Ueber die Leges Edw. Conf.*, 113) believe that the responsi-

rough correspondence of the *borh* association with the tithing, and the obvious advantage of the latter system from a police as well as from a financial point of view, were further influences to make compulsory upon the tithing of the West Saxon shires the duties of suretyship. Elsewhere the vill is to be found in the twelfth century serving as the basis of a frankpledge tithing.[1] The old idea that the fiscal division of Northumbria called the *tenmantale* became a frankpledge tithing is erroneous.[2] In the midlands, however, a manor sometimes answered this purpose;[3] and in East Anglia the local division known as the leet also became a unit for frankpledge suretyship.[4]

Along with this tendency to make suretyship follow territorial lines is also to be traced that tradition of the tithing which called for ten men in a group. When the records first give details in the twelfth century, they show that there might be more than one frankpledge tithing in the same vill or territorial tithing,[5]

bility of the tithing was modelled on that of the hundred. The priority of the fine on the hundred may possibly be shown by the fact that the so-called laws of William represent the murder fine as already in existence (at least in an inchoate state), but speak of *borh* only in the language of the old Saxon law (see Stubbs, *Select Charters*, 84). It is not impossible, however, that the connection of tithing with *borh* suggested the idea of laying the murder fine on the hundred.

[1] "De villata de Wolselee 1/2 m. quia non habuit quem plegiavit" (Salt Archaeol. Soc., *Collections*, iii. 63). The "villata de Morton" (Warwick) paid half a mark "pro libero plegio suo" (*Pipe Roll*, 15 Hen. II, 29). In the shires of Wessex there were frankpledge tithings which bore the names of territorial tithings. See *Pipe Rolls*, 12 Hen. II, 92 (Sussex); 21 Hen. II, 162 (Gloucester); 22 Hen. II, 133 (Berkshire).

[2] See below, pp. 52–53.

[3] *Fridbor* of the lands of Robert (Derby), *Pipe Roll*, 21 Hen. II, 34; frankpledge of the land of Margaret in Aslackby (Lincoln), Hunter, *Pipe Roll*, 1 Ric. I, 66. Ralph the Rustic, a fugitive, dwelt at Rushden (Hertford) in the *franc plege* of the Hospitallers, and the land of the Hospitallers in Rushden was at mercy for his flight (*Rot. Cur. Regis*, ed. Palgrave, i. 159, 10 Ric. I). The land of Alan de Boxle in the vill.of Hoddesdon paid half a mark for a flight (*ibid.* 168).

[4] See Hudson, *Leet Jurisdiction in Norwich*, p. liv.

[5] The phrase "decenne totius villate de Hyate" (Maitland, *Pleas of the*

and thus that, where the population was so large as to form an unwieldy police group, the personal nature of the registration permitted the creation in the hundred court of as many such groups as were deemed convenient. By 1115 there undoubtedly was a basis in actual practice for the assertion that in the vills of the realm men were grouped by tens for purposes of mutual suretyship.[1]

The centralization of administration, which alone could develop and maintain a uniform system of frankpledge, forbids the conclusion that either seigniorial influence or the local financial exactions of Norman officials imparted to the institution its final form. No less than Anglo-Saxon *borh*, its forerunner, does it bear "the imprint of public law."[2] In legal theory and tradition is to be traced the unquestioning assumption of royal direction and supervision. The so-called laws of William, reduced to writing within a generation of his death, ascribe to him the re-enacting of a law of collective *borh*. The *Leges Henrici*, which early in his son's reign represent frankpledge as common to the realm and the legal arrangements for putting men in tithing as uniform, reserve to the king alone cognizance of a breach of *borh*.[3] The thirteenth-century practice of making the enrolment of peasants in frankpledge the occasion for their taking the oath of allegiance to the king,[4] seems to date from

Crown for Gloucester, No. 124) even suggests that in Gloucestershire in 1221 it may have been somewhat unusual for a frankpledge tithing to include the men of a whole vill.

[1] See above, p. 1. This statement undoubtedly holds true much more generally in old Mercia and East Anglia, where the vill proper is the local unit. In the West Saxon shires, where the territorial tithing is the unit, court rolls from first to last show a tendency to make frankpledge follow the territorial unit.

[2] Gross, *Gild Merchant*, i. 180.

[3] *Leges Henrici*, x. 1, in Liebermann, *Gesetze*, i. 556. Cf. "regis multam," in William of Malmesbury, *Gesta Regum* (Rolls Series), i. 130.

[4] See below, p. 130.

Norman days; and the rule of law laid down by Bracton, that the lord cannot remit the view of frankpledge of his men because this right pertains to the king alone,[1] is but the formulation, a century and a half later, of a principle clearly implied in the law of Henry I.[2] By its uniformity, no less than by its rigorous, methodical, exacting nature, frankpledge shows the handiwork of an early Norman king.

The introduction of the legal principles and institutions upon which rested the completed frankpledge system belongs to the early Plantagenet period, just as the definite evolution of frankpledge suretyship belongs to the early Norman period. To the Assize of Clarendon, promulgated a century after the Norman Conquest, are to be ascribed the beginnings of the new order. In this decree King Henry II not only requires that no one receive men into a city or a borough unless they be either in mainpast or in frankpledge,[3] but also enunciates the principle that the supreme right to hold view of frankpledge, even where this is done in a seigniorial court, belongs to the crown, to whose agent, the sheriff, no one either within castle or without, or even in the honor of Wallingford, shall deny access to his court, to the end that before the sheriff all may be put under frankpledge.[4] A far greater and more important innovation resulted from an earlier provision of the same decree which gave to the king's justices in eyre the cognizance of presentments made in the hundred.[5] The effect of this measure was to shift from the sheriff of the county to the itinerant justices of

---

[1] Bracton, fol. 37, i. 290.

[2] "Speciali tamen plenitudine, si opus est, bis in anno conveniant in hundretum suum quicunque liberi, tam heorthfest quam folgarii, ad dinoscendum scilicet inter cetera, si decaniae plenae sint, vel qui quomodo qua ratione recesserint vel super accreverint."—*Leges Henrici*, viii. 1, in Liebermann, *Gesetze*, i. 554.

[3] Assize of Clarendon, ch. x, in Stubbs, *Select Charters*, 144.

[4] Ch. ix.

[5] Ch. i.

the king's central court the function of holding the men of the tithing to the duties for which they were enrolled. The pipe roll of the same year shows the immediate beginning of this control through amercement by the justices, in various counties, of tithings that failed to produce absconding members before them.[1] It was likewise made incumbent upon the justices to amerce a vill for failure to report for enrolment at the sheriff's tourn the names of residents who were out of tithing.[2] Through the eyre the system of frankpledge, which had long been a regalian affair in theory, was thus enforced in franchises no less than in geldable districts, and an instrument of vast importance to the public peace, that had been preserved through local agency, came to be wielded by the king through his personal representatives.

[1] *Pipe Roll*, 12 Hen. II, 9–10, 14, 15, 31, 66, 70, 87, 92.

[2] Thus, for example, in *Pipe Roll*, 23 Hen. II, 200, is the entry, "1/2 m. de villa de Herrefelde quia Ricardus fuit sine plegio."

CHAPTER II

DISTRIBUTION OF FRANKPLEDGE

FRANKPLEDGE presents features remarkable in more ways than one. A system which, to insure the appearance of peasants at trial, organized them into permanent groups, and laid upon the members of these tithings responsibility for each other's custody, is one that by its very nature claims attention. Considered, moreover, as an evidence of strong kingship in that it enlisted the ordinary man in the interest of the general peace, it stands unique in a feudal age. Fully as striking as any other feature, however, is the fact that such a system under such kings was not in force in all parts of the realm.

Frankpledge must, indeed, be characterized as an institution which, though indigenous to English soil, spread neither to districts beyond its original limits in England nor to any non-English region subject to the English king. That it was not prevalent in Normandy seems to be as clear as the fact that it was not of Norman origin.[1] The quo warranto pleas in the thirteenth century make no reference to a view of frankpledge in the islands of Guernsey and Jersey; nor does an assize roll for the Channel Islands in the reign of Edward III, though the latter does mention both the outlawry of fugitives and a part of the leet jurisdiction.[2] There is strong indication that the Anglo-

---

[1] According to Stubbs (*Constitutional History*, i. 96), there is no trace of a similar institution on the Continent prior to the time when it is to be found in full working order in England.

[2] Public Record Office, Assize Roll, No. 1166, 5 Edw. III.

Normans did not carry the system to Ireland; for in the reign of Edward I mainprise or bail appears to have been the only form of suretyship there used for a person accused of crime, even though he were a fugitive.[1] In the laws of the Scottish boroughs also, and in the acts of the Scottish Parliament, *borh* means only warranty or bail.[2] Nor does there seem to have been any frankpledge in Wales; for, as Maitland has shown, the *Statutum Walliae*, in establishing a sheriff's tourn for the newly conquered region, made no provision for the presentments by the heads of tithings which were a distinguishing trait of the English tourn.[3] In Wales these presentments were made instead by all the men of the local court or commote.[4] It is evident, therefore, that the view of frankpledge claimed in Caernarvonshire in 1370 is but the name of a certain jurisdiction,[5] as was the case in England at the same period after the real age of frankpledge was gone.

So uniform has been the operation of the English legal system, even from Norman days, that writers on the English constitution have usually been slow to admit that frankpledge is an important exception to the rule. Indeed, the idea that it was an institution common to the realm of England is presented by legal writers who were perfectly familiar with its workings all about them. The Assize of Clarendon and the Magna Carta of

[1] *Calendar of Justiciary Rolls of Ireland*, 1295–1303 (ed. Mills), 76–77, 166. Coroners' rolls for Ireland fail to call attention to criminals in frankpledge (*ibid.* 175); but in England at this time it was one of the duties of the coroner to keep a record as to what tithing was responsible for a fugitive felon (see Britton, ed. Nichols, i. 13). In Ireland, as in Wales, the sheriff's tourn has no necessary connection with frankpledge (*Calendar of Justiciary Rolls*, 51–52).

[2] See Innes, *Ancient Laws of the Burghs of Scotland*, 57–160.

[3] Maitland, *Select Pleas in Manorial Courts*, p. xxxiii.

[4] *Statutes of the Realm*, i. 57.

[5] *Record of Caernarvon* (Record Com.), 183. Lewis (*Ancient Laws of Wales*, 296) makes a curiously inexact statement when he says that view of frankpledge is not to be found in this record.

1217, in making provision for the maintenance of the system, give no hint that this legislation is not for the whole kingdom.[1] The legal compiler who wrote in the earlier half of the reign of Henry I conveys the impression that frankpledge was everywhere in force;[2] and the idea of William of Malmesbury, who wrote about 1120, is that every Englishman must be in tithing.[3] The person who at some time between 1115 and 1135 collected the so-called *Leges Edwardi Confessoris* explicitly declares that the suretyship of the tithings is for all the vills of the kingdom;[4] and the same idea is to be gained from a reading of Bracton[5] and the law writers of the reign of Edward I.[6] Like some other legal theories, however, this assumption is not literally true, and, so far as any evidence goes to show, never was true, even within the somewhat narrow bounds of Norman England.

That frankpledge suretyship was not required in all parts of England is no new discovery. Three-quarters of a century ago Palgrave found evidence to show that there was none in Shropshire or in Westmoreland, and that the character of records in other northern counties was such as to indicate the absence of the frankpledge tithing.[7] Palgrave did not, however, attempt to determine definitely the limits of the frankpledge region; moreover, by attaching an undue importance to certain evidence pointing to the non-existence of frankpledge in some localities, he was inclined to underrate the prevalence of the system where

---

[1] Stubbs, *Select Charters*, 144, 347; *Statutes of the Realm*, i. 19.

[2] "Communis quippe commodi provida dispensacione statutum est." — *Leges Henrici*, viii. 2, in Liebermann, *Gesetze*, i. 554.

[3] *Gesta Regum* (Rolls Series), i. 129–130.

[4] "Et hoc est, quod de omnibus villis totius regni sub decennali fideiussione debebant omnes esse." — *Leges*, xx. 1, in Liebermann, *Gesetze*, i. 645.

[5] Fol. 124b, ii. 306.

[6] Britton, i. 48; Fleta (1685), 40; *Mirror of Justices* (Selden Soc.), 39.

[7] Palgrave, *Commonwealth*, ii. p. cxxiii, note 32.

it did exist. What remains to be done, then, is to answer as fully as possible two questions: (1) In what counties was there not, and in what counties was there, frankpledge? (2) To what extent did the institution prevail in the frankpledge counties? It will be the aim of this chapter to show that in the period immediately following the Norman Conquest the system in general was not in force in the counties touching the western and northern borders; that it did exist in all of the counties to the south of Yorkshire and to the east of Cheshire, Shropshire, and Herefordshire; and that within the frankpledge region it was a rule to which there were few exceptions.

To prove absolutely that frankpledge was at no time maintained in parts of what had been the border counties of the Conqueror's time is impossible. For some of these counties there is no direct evidence, and for some of the Welsh border counties the evidence is not all on the same side of the question. Yet a silence of the records which elsewhere systematically give details as to the obligations of the tithing, a failure to establish the usual arrangements for keeping up the system, a tendency of medieval law to follow old custom, and, in some instances, the direct testimony of jurors on oath, all taken together go to show with every degree of probability that there was no frankpledge whatever in the old border counties of the north, and, as a rule, none in those of the west.

The lack of evidence, in general a dangerous support for an argument concerning medieval conditions, is in this instance of such a nature as to demand attention. Although royal charters sometimes mention view of frankpledge, documents of this class seem to make not the slightest allusion to such an institution in the Norman border counties, except in a few cases in the west; and the same may be said of the inquisitions post mortem. The hundred and the quo warranto rolls, which, through their

record of private privileges called in question by Edward I,
mention a great many views of frankpledge and frankpledge
tithings in thirty counties, do not refer to anything of the
kind in the old border shires except in Hereford and Shropshire near Wales, — a silence which of itself inclined Maitland
to the view that there was no frankpledge in the northern
counties,[1] and which is certainly very significant from the
fact that in these records this particular right is mentioned
oftenest of all in connection with other counties, and that
even in doubtful ones are to be found companion franchises to
the view of frankpledge along with parts of the ordinary leet
jurisdiction.[2]

Of still greater significance is the failure of records to mention frankpledge in these districts when such an omission would
certainly mean a financial loss to the king were the institution
in force within the county. Thus the pipe rolls, which consist-
ently record amercements laid upon the tithings elsewhere for
non-performance of duty, contain not the slightest allusion to
such a practice in nine western and northern counties. Ordinarily at the end of the thirteenth and the beginning of the
fourteenth century the list of amercements appended to an
assize roll was the most complete record in existence of the
derelictions of frankpledge tithings; yet lists for these doubtful
counties preserved in the Public Record Office contain no
mention whatever of the amercement of a tithing. Since, then,
frankpledge obligation was not here, as elsewhere, one of the
sources of royal revenue at the eyre, it is necessary to assume
either that the system was not in existence in these counties, or,
what is practically impossible, that the royal officials here over-

---

[1] *Select Pleas in Manorial Courts*, p. xxx, note 1.

[2] The enforcement of the assize of bread and beer is mentioned in Cumberland. See *Plac. de Quo War.*, 129, 371, 375, 379; also *Northumberland Assize
Rolls* (Surtees Soc.), 357–358.

looked a considerable source of revenue which everywhere else they fully exploited.

But not alone in entries touching financial matters is there a failure to mention frankpledge in the records of the royal courts for the extreme north and west. Although the assize rolls, which were kept for every county in England in the period from the reign of Henry III to that of Edward III, show the regular enforcement of frankpledge suretyship in the great body of counties, they have nothing to say about tithing or frankpledge suretyship in the nine doubtful ones. In the light of conditions which these rolls often reveal, this is a fact of far greater import than at first sight appears. In 1256, and again in 1279, the itinerant justices held criminal pleas for Northumberland, the records of which show a deplorable state of the public peace in that county. Practically all malefactors fled across the Scottish border, or to Durham, or to lesser liberties within the county, and thus escaped with the mild penalty of being proclaimed outlaws. Here, if anywhere, frankpledge was needed, and here, if anywhere, one would expect to find it in full operation; yet in an account fairly bristling with flights of fugitives, abjurations of the realm, confiscations of criminals' chattels, and other penalties in great detail, to which is appended a list of amercements before the justices, there is not a word to suggest that a tithing was held responsible for not producing one of its members.[1] In the other doubtful counties the silence of the records is just as convincing. Palgrave, after examining assize rolls for the northern counties, doubted from their tenor whether any entry relating to collective frankpledge could be found in this class of material, which elsewhere affords the best account of frankpledge activity;[2] and since he wrote no dis-

---

[1] *Northumberland Assize Rolls*, pp. xviii, xix, 70 ff., 374 ff.
[2] Palgrave, *Commonwealth*, ii. p. cxxiii, note 32.

covery has tended to weaken the powerful conviction created
by the silence of these records. Not only in Northumberland,
but in Cumberland, Westmoreland, Lancashire, and Yorkshire, the assize rolls, through their failure to mention either the
ordinary obligation of the tithing or its amercement for default
in that obligation, show that it was not the practice for itinerant
justices to enforce frankpledge in these as in other counties.
Furthermore, an examination of similar rolls in western counties
proves the same fact for Shropshire and Herefordshire.[1]

The machinery for the maintenance of frankpledge was quite
clearly not in operation in the greater number of the counties
where the system has not yet been found. The division of the
four northernmost counties into wards rather than hundreds
was not designed to provide for the usual administration of
frankpledge through view in a hundred court. The sheriff's
tourn, which since 1166 had been charged with this duty,[2]
seems not to have been introduced into the north till a later
date, in imitation of an institution found useful elsewhere. Thus
in Northumberland it was first held about the middle of the
thirteenth century, and then contrary to the custom of the
county, an encroachment which led Henry III to remit the right
by charter.[3] In Durham the first account of the institution

---

[1] Among the rolls in the Public Record Office which show this most clearly
are Assize Rolls, Nos. 133 (Cumberland), 300 C (Herefordshire), 409 (Lancashire), 739 (Shropshire), 986 (Westmoreland), and 1057 and 1101 (Yorkshire). In the county palatine of Durham, assize rolls of the reign of Henry III
which deal with criminal affairs (No. 223) preserve the same silence as to
frankpledge. The records of the Cheshire palatinate show quite clearly that
in the time of Edward III tithings were not held responsible for escape of
fugitives (for the period 15–31 Edward III, see Public Record Office, Chester
Eyre Rolls, Nos. 13, 14). At so late a date, however, a similar silence is to be
expected even in frankpledge counties.

[2] Assize of Clarendon, ch. ix, in Stubbs, *Select Charters*, 144.

[3] *Northumberland Assize Rolls*, 163–164; *Rot. Hundred.*, ii. 19, 21; Public
Record Office, *List of Sheriffs for England and Wales*, 97.

comes from the fourteenth century;[1] in Lancashire there had been no tourn of the county prior to the time of Henry III;[2] and even in Yorkshire, as will be shown later, there was none as late as 1293. The failure, moreover, of the hundred and the quo warranto rolls to mention view of frankpledge in Lancashire and Yorkshire and the counties to the north tends strongly to show that in franchises, as well as elsewhere in these doubtful counties, there were no regular administrative arrangements for keeping up frankpledge tithings.

The absence of the sheriff's tourn, as well as the failure of the itinerant justices to have frankpledge suretyship enforced in counties outside those in which the activity is regularly recorded, may be taken to indicate the exclusion of the institution from the extreme north and west not only in the thirteenth century but also in the twelfth. This is an easy inference from a thirteenth-century interpretation of the Great Charter. In 1269 the people of Northumberland successfully appealed to the absence of the sheriff's tourn from their county when the charter was issued as exempting them from that provision of the re-issue of 1217 which allowed the sheriff twice annually to make the usual round of the county.[3] As the full article required the sheriff to make view of frankpledge at his fall tourn, that the tithings might be maintained through the same pecuniary penalties as in the time of Henry II,[4] it seems obvious that there was no frankpledge in Northumberland prior to the death of Henry II in 1189; and the facts already presented warrant the same statement as to Lancashire and Durham, and apparently for Westmoreland and Cumberland as well. This appeal to

---

[1] Lapsley, *County Palatine of Durham*, 195, 331.

[2] *Plac. de Quo War.*, 371.

[3] *Northumberland Assize Rolls*, 163–164.

[4] Magna Carta of 1217, ch. xlii, *Statutes of the Realm*, i. 19; Stubbs, *Select Charters*, 347.

Magna Carta also has a bearing on the case of every county from the records of which frankpledge is missing. What it means is this, — that, wherever frankpledge existed in the time of the sons and the grandson of Henry II, there, according to the legal presumption, it existed in his own time. If the contrary can be proved, the frankpledge system cannot legally be maintained. The clause of Magna Carta requiring that tourn, view of frankpledge, and tithing be maintained "as was wont" establishes these institutions on the basis of conditions as they existed during the reign of the first Plantagenet king. Counties with no sheriff's tourn and no frankpledge after the issuance of the Great Charter had none at least a quarter of a century before 1215; and suspicions as to the absence of frankpledge in counties as to which the pipe rolls of Henry II are significantly silent may justly be recalled when in the reigns of Henry III and Edward I the silence of other records engenders like suspicions.

Indirect evidence and inference, irresistible though they appear in some cases, are not the only testimony in support of the thesis that frankpledge was not an institution of the old border counties of the eleventh and twelfth centuries. In the last half of the thirteenth century it was the practice for the jurors representing a county to declare before the itinerant justices what customs, generally observed elsewhere, were not in force within their county, so that they might not be held responsible for the non-observance of them. Were there a complete set of the assize rolls, it is possible that they would settle the question by categorical statement in regard to every doubtful county except the palatinates of Durham and Chester; but, unfortunately, there are direct, authoritative statements of this kind for only three counties. Two of these rolls, as already hinted, Palgrave discovered and printed, — those for Shropshire and Westmoreland.[1] The Shropshire jurors for 1256 declared that there was neither murder fine nor tithing in their county;[2] and the Westmoreland jurors for 1292 likewise bore testimony that in Westmoreland there was no Englishry presentment, no murder fine, no tithing, no view of frankpledge, and no mainpast, adding, for the sake of emphasis, a further declaration to the effect that none of these institutions had ever existed in the northern regions beyond the Trent. As to the truth of this casual remark, made for the purpose of carrying weight with the justices, there can now be scarcely the shadow of a doubt if one but assumes with thirteenth-century writers that by the Trent River is meant its confluence with the Humber rather than its general course. The jurors simply intended to give the southern boundary of Yorkshire as the northern frankpledge limit.[3]

The great objection that has always been made to the acceptance of this testimony of the Westmoreland jurors is that it conflicts with a well-known passage concerning Yorkshire in the *Leges Edwardi Confessoris*,[4] where frankpledge is represented as in existence among the Eboracenses, who call it *ten manne tale*, or the number of ten men.[5] Pollock and Maitland, however, reject the authority of the *Leges*, though they question the accuracy of the declaration concerning the line of the Trent.[6] It is the statement of the *Leges* and not that

---

[1] See Palgrave, *Commonwealth*, ii. p. cxxiii, note 32; also above, p. 44.

[2] The absence of the murder fine from the pipe rolls of the twelfth century seems to substantiate this assertion.

[3] A reference to the inquests post mortem of the north and midlands will easily show that this is the usual legal sense wherever *citra* or *ultra Trentam* occurs.

[4] Ch. xx, in Liebermann, *Gesetze*, i. 645; Thorpe, *Laws*, i. 450; Schmid, *Gesetze*, 502.

[5] Palgrave, *Commonwealth*, ii. pp. cxxiii–cxxiv.

[6] *English Law* (1895), i. 556.

of the jurors which must be rejected. Bishop Stubbs makes it
clear that the pecuniary exaction in the north known as *tenmantale* resembled Danegeld rather than any payment connected with frankpledge.[1]   One of the charters to Rievaulx
definitely affirms that they are the same;[2] and there are other
charters that grant quittance both of *tenmantale* and of frankpledge, as if the two were regarded as altogether different.[3]
The *tenmantale* itself, as Vinogradoff has shown, was but a unit
of land measure, a carucate of ten *mantales* or tofts, the holding
of ten men.[4]   The compiler of the *Leges*, who seems to have
been an ecclesiastic of foreign birth resident in Warwickshire,[5]
was evidently misled by the fact that in the somewhat distant
region of Yorkshire there was a reckoning of men by tens, and
concluded that this meant the presence of the suretyship tithing.
A third assize roll, which Palgrave did not discover, and which
has not before been brought to light in this connection, sets the
question at rest so far as Yorkshire is concerned; for in 1293
the jurors at the eyre had it recorded in the usual way that no
Englishry was presented in the county, that there was no murder fine, tithing, or frankpledge, that no view of frankpledge or
tourn of sheriff was held there,[6] and that there was no mainpast

[1] Roger of Hovedon, *Chronica* (Rolls Series), iii. 242, note 1.

[2] *Chartulary of Rievaulx* (Surtees Soc.), 142.

[3] *Ibid.* 184; Turton, *Honor and Forest of Pickering* (North Riding Record
Soc.), iv. 71–72.

[4] Vinogradoff, *English Society in the Eleventh Century*, 103, note 1; Gale,
Register of the Honor of Richmond, 22.

[5] Liebermann, *Ueber die Leges Edw. Conf.*, 17–18. Liebermann (*ibid.* 31) inclines to the view that this payment is identical with that known as view of
frankpledge, and also understands the Eboracenses as referring to the inhabitants of the whole ecclesiastical province of York, thus assuming the existence
of frankpledge throughout the north generally. The whole theory falls with
the story of the *tenmantale*.

[6] The tourn in the north seems to have been but a seigniorial affair which
had to do only with the holdings of one lord. Some surprise has been expressed
that the tourn at Wakefield (Yorkshire Archaeol. Soc., *Record Series*, xxxvi.

obligation for which any one ought to respond.[1] The familiar account of the tenmantale, like some other parts of the laws of the twelfth century, must be classed as pure legend.

As to the Welsh border, unquestionable evidence leads to the conclusion that in two of the three English counties frankpledge was not regularly maintained as a county institution, although by the middle of the thirteenth century the view of frankpledge, and possibly frankpledge itself, had found its way into franchises. For the third county, the palatinate of Chester, the evidence in the real frankpledge period (prior to 1340) is insufficient to warrant a decision either for or against the existence of the institution.[2] One can only reason from general similarity of conditions that the surety system of Cheshire was probably not different from that of the county palatinate of Durham,[3] or from that of the adjoining counties of Lancashire and Shropshire. For the last-named county the direct state-

p. xi) had nothing to do with frankpledge. The assize roll of 1293 solves the problem.

[1] Public Record Office, Assize Roll, No. 1098, 21 Edw. I.

[2] The court leet existed in Manchester and in other parts of the county of Lancaster, as well as in Cheshire, when in the fourteenth century frankpledge was on the decline. There has been an attempt to show that the leet was an ancient institution in these two counties (see Crofton, in Lancashire and Cheshire Antiq. Soc., *Transactions*, v. 137); but this attempt depends largely upon the theory, since discredited by Maitland (*Select Pleas in Manorial Courts*, Introd.), that the leet was an ancient court. No clear case for the existence of these courts in the real age of frankpledge has been made out. They simply follow a form for manorial leets which had become common, without having any features traceable to frankpledge (Hudson, *Leet Jurisdiction in Norwich*, p. lxxii, note). Such views of frankpledge in the reign of Edward III are to be found not only in Cheshire (Salt Archaeol. Soc., *Collections*, xvi. 15, 17; Public Record Office, Chester Quo Warranto Rolls, No. 1, mm. 2–8), but also in Wales (*Record of Caernarvon*, 183), where frankpledge itself never existed (Maitland, *Select Pleas in Manorial Courts*, p. xxxiii).

[3] General regulations for the maintenance of the peace seem to have been similar in the two counties. See Lapsley, *County Palatine of Durham*, 221, 226–227.

ment already given is conclusive. The failure of assize rolls to mention frankpledge both here and in Herefordshire is sufficient to prove that the royal officials were not charged with its enforcement. A thirteenth-century record in the *Red Book of the Exchequer* shows, furthermore, that in the county of Hereford no revenues from the usual payment known as view of frankpledge were received by the crown,[1] a fact which, in view of the general prevalence of such a payment in frankpledge counties, indicates that there was no view by the sheriff here, just as there was none in counties farther north. In 1284, however, the city of Hereford had "of old" held view of frankpledge "without interruption of their lords";[2] and in 1303 a jury found that the lord of the manor of Albrighton in Shropshire had from legal memory held view of his burgesses.[3] There are also on record a few instances in which lords claimed view of frankpledge for given vills or manors in these counties; but the fact that the information comes in the main from the quo warranto pleas shows that there was something about these claims which the king's attorneys held to be irregular.[4] It is well known that the nobility along the marches often, and especially before the conquest of Wales, enjoyed a privileged position, with unusual liberties in their own domains;[5] and it is certain that these pleas for the Welsh border region in the time of Edward I represent here as elsewhere an effort on the part of the king to reduce unwarranted privileges claimed by pre-

---

[1] Rolls Series, ii. 777.

[2] Matthews, *Cardiff Records*, i. 14.

[3] Eyton, *Shropshire*, ii. 156.

[4] In 1292 Earl Humphrey Bohun claimed view of frankpledge for three vills in Hereford (*Plac. de Quo War.*, 273). In the next year John le Strange claimed the same privilege at Cheswardine in Shropshire by charter of Henry II, but was unsuccessful in establishing his title, since his charter did not convey the right in specific terms (Eyton, *Shropshire*, x. 33).

[5] Duncumb, *Hereford*, i. 80–81.

scription.[1] Whatever may have been the innovations introduced through seigniorial influence, the Shropshire assize roll of 1256 and the Herefordshire roll of 1257 show clearly enough, in presenting their lists of amercements, that frankpledge was not regularly enforced in these counties.

As a general surety system, frankpledge depended upon control by royal officials in tourn and in eyre; but outside the thirty frankpledge counties direction by either one or both of these agencies was lacking. A failure of the assize rolls to mention frankpledge in the usual connection, and a failure both of these records and of the pipe rolls to record the ordinary amercements for delinquency of tithings in producing criminals, show that the itinerant justices did not enforce the frankpledge obligation in the old border counties. The non-existence of the regular sheriff's tourn in Lancashire, Yorkshire, and the counties farther north left no regular means of maintaining the tithings in those counties; and the general situation in Cheshire, the failure of the exchequer to collect view of frankpledge in Herefordshire, and the evidence of jurors on oath in Shropshire, all point to a similar state of affairs. In Yorkshire the testimony of jurors bears out that of other jurors in Westmoreland, to the effect that there was frankpledge neither in their own county nor in any of the region north of the Trent, a statement which must now be accepted as the expression of a fact well known at

---

[1] In 1203 there was a hundred in Shropshire, held by William Fitz Alan, which owed no suit at the county court (its men never coming before the justices or the sheriff for death or burning or on any summons), and within the bounds of which, according to the witness of the whole county, no grand assize had ever been held (Shropshire Archaeol. and Nat. Hist. Soc., *Transactions*, 2d series, xi. 249). In 1265 a royal charter acquitting of view of frankpledge tenants at Cainham and Walton in Shropshire and at Shobdon in Hereford, who held their estates by gift of the De Mortimers (*Calendar of Charter Rolls*, ii. 56), suggests that one of this famous name had conferred an unusual right which the king at that time felt bound to respect.

the end of the thirteenth century. Since Magna Carta stood as a legal barrier to the introduction of the system in places where it had not existed in the reign of Henry II, the conclusion follows that in eight, and probably in nine, English counties frankpledge suretyship was not a county institution either in the twelfth century or in succeeding ones.[1]

Why frankpledge, which was considered of transcendent importance by Norman and Plantagenet kings, was not maintained uniformly throughout England is an interesting question. The limits of the frankpledge district had apparently been established by the reign of Henry I in the first third of the twelfth century,[2] and had been perpetuated by Magna Carta as they stood in the reign of Henry II near the end of that century. The absence of the institution in the northernmost counties is thus easily explained, for at the Norman Conquest most of these districts were either Scottish dependencies or else in a semi-independent state.[3] The progress of Norman arms here was slow; it was, indeed, not till after an alienation to Scotland by Stephen and a re-conquest by Henry II that all this region was finally attached to the English crown.[4] In the parts of the border districts continuously retained after 1066 the absence of frankpledge is accounted for by the crude and unsettled state of administration at that time. As to Yorkshire and

---

[1] The doubtful county is Cheshire (see above, p. 53, and note 2). The views of frankpledge found in townships and manors of Durham and North Durham, in the borough of Durham, and in Berwick-on-Tweed in the sixteenth and seventeenth centuries (see, for example, Raine, *North Durham*, 20, and App., 152), are quite clearly later jurisdictions having no connection with actual frankpledge. Similar rights are to be found in Yorkshire in the same period (Stubbs, *Constitutional History*, i. 95, note 4).

[2] See below, pp. 59–60.

[3] See Tout, in Poole's *Historical Atlas of Modern Europe*, XVIII.

[4] *Pipe Rolls of Cumberland, Westmorland, and Durham* (Newcastle Soc. of Antiquaries), pp. xiv, xv, xix, xxii; Wilson, *Victoria History of Cumberland*, i. 309–310.

Cheshire, which between them originally included Lancashire, and as to Shropshire and Hereford, the problem is not so easily solved.

On the Welsh border one almost expects to find something of the same lack of institutional development as on the Scottish;[1] but that in Yorkshire, which had been so unruly that the Conqueror had found it necessary mercilessly to lay waste a great part of the county,[2] his son and his great-grandson should have failed to maintain a surety system as strict as that to be found elsewhere is somewhat surprising. One explanation is probably to be found in the fact that in Norman days Yorkshire was a border county, where border conditions no doubt tended to make it impossible for local courts to enforce the usual measures for the maintenance of the peace. It seems to have been a continuance of the same state of affairs that in the thirteenth century brought both Yorkshire and Lancashire under the influence of the border jurisdiction of the marches.[3]

The ultimate reason, however, for the absence of frankpledge in the border counties of Norman days is to be found in the considerable degree of local administrative autonomy enjoyed by

---

[1] In the pipe rolls of the twelfth century the county of Hereford is designated as Herefordshire in Wales. Conditions here were such as to demand a modification of the usual rule concerning outlaws. According to Bracton (fol. 128, ii. 338–339), an outlaw might be killed at any time in the counties of Hereford and Gloucester near the march of Wales; elsewhere he could be killed with impunity only when he defended himself or attempted flight. It is also to be remembered that the situation was so troublesome in this region that the Conqueror did not try to control it himself, but by creating palatinates in Cheshire and Shropshire turned it over wholly to powerful nobles. See Ormerod, *Cheshire*, i. 9, 145; Stubbs, *Constitutional History*, i. 294; Eyton, *Shropshire*, i. 22, note 2; 70, note 198; 242.

[2] See Ramsay, *Foundations of England*, ii. 73.

[3] Lapsley, in *Amer. Hist. Review*, v. 441. In Lancashire (Tait, *Manchester*, 153), and probably in other counties without frankpledge, there were so few Normans in the reign of William the Conqueror that such an institution was not necessary for their protection.

these regions during the preceding period, an independence that
prevented the establishment of the Anglo-Saxon *borh* system,
the foundation upon which frankpledge was erected. For the
old kingdom of Northumbria — the present Yorkshire and the
region to the north — this explanation seems to be particularly
true; for the laws of Athelstan show that this ruler experienced
no little difficulty in enforcing his *borh* regulations in his own
West Saxon districts.[1]   But Athelstan, despite his great victory
of Brunanburh, did not succeed in wresting Northumbria entirely
from the control of the Danes, who had hitherto held it. Successive rebellions under native kings for two decades more make it
certain that regular Anglo-Saxon administration could not have
been established until in 958 Edgar "succeeded to the kingdom
as well of the West Saxons as of the Mercians and Northum-
brians." [2]   Even during the reign of this strong king, Oslac, the
earl of the last-named people, seems to have been nearly independent,[3] and the right of the Danish parts of England to have
"as good laws as they best may choose " [4] was especially conceded. Although Edgar expressly declared that every man
whether within or without the cities should be in *borh*,[5] the control of his weak successors could not have been such as to enable
them to force this innovation upon the population of the wild
and semi-independent north. During the reigns of Edward the
Confessor and Harold, earls Siward and Tostig, in an earldom
now limited to Yorkshire,[6] showed the same spirit of independence as their predecessors, the latter noble even setting aside

---

[1] 5 Athelstan, Prol., 3; 4 Athelstan, ii, iii. 2: Liebermann, *Gesetze*, i. 166–
167, 171.

[2] *Anglo-Saxon Chronicle* (Rolls Series), ii. 92.

[3] Green, *Conquest of England*, 325–328.

[4] 4 Edgar, ii. 1, xii, in Liebermann, *Gesetze*, i. 210–213 *passim*.

[5] 4 Edgar, iii, *ibid.* 210–211.

[6] Through alienation of territory to Scotland. See Green, *Conquest of
England*, 471.

the laws of Canute.[1] Green declares that on the eve of the
Conquest no king's writ ran in the Northumbria of Siward;[2]
and Ramsay is equally positive that the same was true to the
west of a line drawn from the Humber to Bristol Channel and
the mouth of the Exe.[3] The failure of the king's authority in
precisely those regions where frankpledge was never developed
thus becomes an illuminating fact.

To prove that the frankpledge system was in force in each of
the thirty counties from the south of Yorkshire to the southern
coast of England, and from the North Sea to Land's End and
the Welsh border, there is convincing evidence. An examination of the printed hundred and quo warranto rolls shows that
view of frankpledge — the session of court which had the duty
of putting in tithing those who were liable to its obligations —
is mentioned in every one of these counties in the reign of
Edward I. In the Public Record Office there are assize rolls for
all but two of these counties, which show that in the same reign
itinerant justices systematically enforced the obligation of the
tithing by a pecuniary penalty in case of default. For the two
counties, Derby and Nottingham, the records of which are wanting for this period, there are rolls for the opening years of the
reign of Edward III that establish the fact of the same enforcement of the obligation.

Within this region, moreover, the regular maintenance of
frankpledge antedated the reign of Edward I by more than a
century. According to the twenty-three pipe rolls of Henry II,
from 1166 to the end of the reign, in twenty-nine of the counties
amercements were laid before the justices in eyre upon tithings
which had failed to produce offending members as required by

---

[1] A circumstance which Page (in *Archaeologia*, li. pt. i. 145) believes points to
a continuance of the Northumbrian witan to so late a date.

[2] *Conquest of England*, 492, 561.

[3] *Foundations of England*, ii. 22.

law. Not only is frankpledge to be found in the thirtieth county, Cambridge, in the reign of Edward I, as just shown, but the joint pipe roll of this county with Huntingdon for the ninth year of Richard I, containing mention of not fewer than nine frankpledge cases, makes it reasonably certain that even in the reign of Henry II Cambridge, no less than the counties round about it, had the system; and even for a still earlier time it is possible to find indication of the same distribution. In view of the persistence with which William of Malmesbury and the *leges* of the first half of the twelfth century present the idea that the law of frankpledge was for the kingdom as a whole, there need be little hesitancy in affirming that, at least as early as the reign of Henry I, the institution was in force throughout that compact portion of England in which, as the records show, the frankpledge tithing was maintained from the age of Henry II to that of Edward III.[1]

As to the prevalence of the frankpledge obligation in the various townships of the thirty counties it is of course possible to speak only in general terms. An enactment of Henry II in 1166 declares that no one, whether within or without a castle, shall prevent a sheriff from entering his court and land to make view of frankpledge, in order that all may be in suretyship and put under frankpledge before the sheriff.[2] That there were in the thirteenth century a few communities exempt from this requirement even in districts where frankpledge was the rule has long been known; but it does not appear that these exemptions were so numerous as was formerly supposed. Quittance

---

[1] A charter grant of Henry I, dating somewhere between 1114 and 1129 and directed to the sheriffs of all counties in which the abbot of St. Edmunds had lands, forbade the men of St. Edmunds to go out of their own soke "pro plegiis suis et friborgis et treingis renovandis aliter quam facere solebant" (*Eng. Hist. Review*, xxiv. 427).

[2] Assize of Clarendon, ch. ix, in Stubbs, *Select Charters*, 144.

of frankpledge in royal charters prior to the time of Edward I seems usually to have been interpreted by the grantee as a concession from the king of the right to hold view of frankpledge and to enjoy its profits.[1] Even when charters specify that tenants in a given place are exempt from frankpledge, reference is probably to the payment by that name and not to frankpledge suretyship. Grants exempting both from frankpledge and from view of frankpledge [2] suggest merely the transfer of the payment and the jurisdiction from royal to seigniorial hands. The number of actual immunities was therefore probably much smaller than a reading of charters would seem to show.

The most prominent examples of the exemption of communities from the duties of the tithing have hitherto been sought in certain boroughs; but, since boroughs often had unusual privileges, such cases need not be regarded as significant. Of Bristol, Worcester, and Ilchester it is recorded that in the early thirteenth century they had no frankpledge; [3] but Bristol and Ilchester had views of frankpledge about half a century later,[4] and there is some reason for supposing that in these two cases the entries in the rolls are to be understood as showing merely that there was no frankpledge with which the royal officials had to do.[5] Henry II decreed that no one in a city or a borough

---

[1] Pollock and Maitland, *English Law* (1895), i. 565, and note 1.

[2] As in Dugdale, *Monasticon*, vii. 931.

[3] Palgrave, *Commonwealth*, ii. p. cxxiii, note 32; Healey, *Somersetshire Pleas* (Somerset Record Soc.), 85.

[4] *Plac. de Quo War.*, 246, 690; Seyer, *Charters of Bristol*, 34.

[5] Watson, *Pleas of the Crown for Bristol*, 1221, p. 104. According to the record (*ibid.* 136), the court appears loath to accept the statement of the jurors, declaring that "it must be discussed." In 1243 the bailiffs of Ilchester plead that according to royal charter they are not to answer beyond the walls of the town (Healey, *Somersetshire Pleas*, 210). In the borough of Tavistock the sheriff appears to have held tourn only before the royal charter was granted (*Rot. Hundred.*, i. 81).

should have or receive men in his house or his soke or on his land unless such persons were either in his mainpast or in frankpledge.[1] A writer in the time of John shows that the municipal ward had an organization which corresponded to frankpledge;[2] and the word ward often appears in assize rolls as an equivalent of the word tithing. The assertion in a statute of 1473 that most of the boroughs and towns of substance within the realm had leets and views of frankpledge,[3] though not positive evidence for the existence of such courts and for their enforcement of frankpledge two or three centuries earlier, is of considerable assistance in forming conclusions for the age of frankpledge. Whatever may have been the grounds for the exemption of some boroughs from the control of the king's justices in the time of Henry III, there can be no question of the fact that in the reign of Edward I cities and boroughs had in many cases to answer at the eyre for matters relating to suretyship just as did ordinary vills,[4] and that in a growing town still subject to

---

[1] Assize of Clarendon, ch. x, in Stubbs, *Select Charters*, 144.

[2] Liebermann, *Consiliatio Cnuti*, 13; Palgrave, *Commonwealth*, ii. p. cxxv, note 34.

[3] *Statutes of the Realm*, ii. 442.

[4] As shown by the assize rolls in the Public Record Office for the period between 1279 and 1302, the more prominent places which had a responsibility concerning frankpledge before the itinerant justices were the following: borough of Northampton, Assize Roll, No. 620, mm. 76–77; vill of Coventry, No. 956, m. 46; boroughs of Dudley and Kidderminster, No. 1026, m. 38, and borough of Pershore, m. 38b; vill of Bedford, No. 12, m. 29b, and vill of Dunstable, m. 32b; borough of Abingdon, No. 43, m. 27; borough of Reading, No. 46, m. 31; boroughs of Bodmin and Helston, No. 118; city of Canterbury, No. 376, m. 62, and city of Rochester, m. 66b; London, — vill of Westminster, No. 554, m. 64, ward of Aldersgate, No. 547, m. 3, ward of Faringdon, m. 6, ward of Billingsgate, m. 18, and ward of Cripplegate, m. 30; the borough within the walls of Oxford, No. 708, m. 41, and borough of Banbury, m. 47b; borough of Newcastle, No. 804, m. 58; borough of Southwark, No. 876, m. 42b; city of Chichester, No. 926, m. 27b, and borough of Arundel, m. 21b; borough of Chippenham, No. 1001, m. 16, borough of Malmesbury, m. 44b, borough of Wilton, m. 61, city of Sarum, m. 62, and borough of Marlborough, m. 66.

a feudal lord this requirement was likely to be the rule. In conclusion it may be said on this point that, although town records are often wanting for the frankpledge period, as well as for later times, such records as there are indicate that what is said of the court leet in the fifteenth century may be said of frankpledge itself in the thirteenth, — that it was found in most of the towns of England.[1]

Besides some few boroughs and districts that may have been specifically exempted by royal charter, there were, according to the records, two other classes of places in frankpledge counties in which the system was wanting. One of these categories included certain forests. Thus, in 1221 there was no tithing suretyship in the forest of Dean in Gloucestershire,[2] though a certain forester at Westbury is spoken of as being not only in frankpledge but at the head of a tithing as well.[3] In forest pleas elsewhere frankpledge is mentioned in the usual way.[4] In the other class of places the system had existed but had become extinct, a fact that is to be attributed not so much to laxness in main-

[1] Besides those named above, the following are also mentioned: Bristol and Tetbury (*Plac. de Quo War.*, 259); Gloucester (Maitland, *Pleas of the Crown for Gloucester*, No. 450; Atkyns, *Gloucestershire*, 60); Tewkesbury (*Plac. de Quo War.*, 246); Derby, Lichfield, and Burton-on-Trent (Cox and Markham, *Records of Northampton*, ii. 141–142); Nottingham (Stevenson, *Records of Nottingham*, i. 66); Leicester (Bateson, *Records of Leicester*, i. 365, ii. 153); Huntingdon (Griffith, *Records of Huntingdon*, 20); Hertford (*Rot. Hundred.*, i. 194); Wycombe (*ibid.* 34); Shaftesbury (Mayo, *Records of Shaftesbury*, 17); Calne (Marsh, *Calne*, 24, 34; *Rot. Hundred.*, ii. 236); Winchester (Kitchin, *Charter of Edward III to St. Giles Fair*, 34); Windsor (*Plac. de Quo War.*, 82); Wallingford (Hedges, *Wallingford*, i. 316, ii. 10–11); Guildford (*Plac. de Quo War.*, 743; Gross, *Gild Merchant*, ii. 94); Norwich (Public Record Office, Pipe Roll, 32 Hen. II, Norfolk); Ipswich (*Black Book of the Admiralty*, Rolls Series, ii. 130–131); Yarmouth (Merewether and Stephens, *Boroughs and Municipal Corporations*, ii. 755–757); Bury St. Edmunds (Gross, *Gild Merchant*, ii. 33; *Chron. Jocelinide Brakelonda*, Camden Soc., 74); Colchester (Harrod, *Court Rolls of Colchester*, 8).

[2] Maitland, *Pleas of the Crown for Gloucester*, No. 183.

[3] *Ibid.* No. 315. See below, p. 89.

[4] Turner, *Select Pleas of the Forest*, 71.

taining tithings, as to the removal of tenants from a manor where they had formerly lived, and to their consequent inability to keep up the tithing which they had constituted. An example of this situation is found in 1324 on the abbot of Burton's manor of " Huncyndon " in Derbyshire.[1]

In view of the facts just presented, the oft-repeated assertion of Palgrave that frankpledge did not exist in portions of the counties lying in the former kingdoms of Wessex and Mercia must be regarded as misleading.[2] The presumption is that this form of suretyship was maintained generally in the thirty counties, except where there happened to be one of the peculiar conditions above mentioned. The usual thirteenth-century assumption that a quittance of frankpledge by the king conveyed authority to a lord or a corporation to maintain the system, was based on the idea that suretyship of the tithing was an institution of general importance which must be sustained by local agency if not by royal power. The Great Charter of 1217, as already noted, regarded it as prevailing generally, and directed sheriffs to make view of frankpledge in the accustomed manner, that tithings might be kept intact and the king's peace maintained. Bracton goes even beyond the broad ground of his predecessors in declaring that every man of the required classes shall be in frankpledge or in mainpast.[3] Such assertions alone militate against the theory that any considerable number of communities within the frankpledge bounds were without the suretyship of tithings.

Conclusive evidence against it, however, seems to be found in

---

[1] Salt Archaeol. Soc., *Collections*, v. pt. i. 87. Huncyndon is probably Hunsdon. The absence of frankpledge from the vill of Killcot in Gloucester in 1221 may have been due to negligence. At any rate, the whole vill was fined for the flight of a murderer (Maitland, *Pleas of the Crown for Gloucester*, No. 364).

[2] See Palgrave, *Commonwealth*, i. 196, 203; ii. p. cxxiii.

[3] Fol. 124b, ii. 306.

the hundred and the quo warranto rolls. One result of the
inquiry represented in these registers and of the pleas based
upon it is that the records, so far as they have been preserved,
contain the names of all the hundreds, boroughs, hamlets, vills,
and manors for which in the reign of Edward I view of frankpledge was held by any one except the king's officers. Since,
according to Magna Carta and the practice of Henry II, this
view was to be made regularly by the sheriff, the performance
of the function by private persons, although of frequent occurrence, is, at least from the legal point of view, to be regarded as
the exception rather than the rule. Yet such instances are surprisingly numerous in these rolls. Not only are practically all
of the views mentioned in private hands, but in only six of the
thirty regular counties are there less than ten of them; while
nine counties have between ten and fifty, six between fifty and
a hundred, and nine more than a hundred. Norfolk leads the
list with more than two hundred and fifty, and the small counties
of Huntingdon and Bedford have respectively in the neighborhood of a hundred and ten and a hundred and forty-five. The
little county of Rutland alone has about twenty. Derby, Northampton, and Nottingham, counties for which this series of
records hardly ever mentions view of frankpledge, have a good
many views in the quo warranto rolls of Edward III. The number of communities in each county for which, as shown by the
published rolls, view of frankpledge was held in the time of
Edward I is indicated in the table on the next page.

Fortunately, one is able to supplement the results of this
count by the use of other records, so that conclusions need not
rest wholly upon the accidental circumstance of usurpation here
and there of what Edward I considered his rights. The assize
rolls and the pipe rolls show that it was the custom of the itinerant justices to enforce the frankpledge obligation throughout

View of Frankpledge in Hundred and Quo Warranto Rolls.

	County.	Bor-oughs.	Ham-lets.	Vills.	Manors.	Other communities and un-specified ones.	Total number of com-muni-ties.
1	Bedford . . .	..	1	4	15	126	146
2	Berks	1	..	..	..	11	12
3	Buckingham .	1	2	11	31	84	129
4	Cambridge . .	..	1	28	2	118	149
5	Cornwall . . .	..	..	..	7	3	10
6	Derby	..	..	..	7	...	7
7	Devon	..	..	..	3	75	78
8	Dorset	..	..	..	1	1	2
9	Essex	..	..	4	..	93	97
10	Gloucester . .	1	1	7	40	89	138
11	Hampshire . .	..	..	..	3	...	3
12	Hereford [1] . .	..	..	..	..	3	3
13	Hertford . . .	1	10	1	8	38	58
14	Huntingdon .	..	..	26	24	62	112
15	Kent	..	..	9	7	55	71
16	Leicester . . .	..	..	..	..	12	12
17	Lincoln . . .	..	..	93	13	68	174
18	Middlesex . .	..	..	3	6	49	58
19	Norfolk . . .	..	..	59	5	194	258
20	Northampton .	..	..	..	..	16	16
21	Nottingham .	..	..	..	1	..	1
22	Oxford . . .	..	3	7	11	36	57
23	Rutland . . .	..	..	1	..	20	21
24	Somerset . . .	1	..	..	3	30	34
25	Stafford . . .	..	..	1	6	6	13
26	Suffolk . . .	1	..	5	7	137	150
27	Surrey	1	..	4	11	12	28
28	Sussex	..	..	3	6	15	24
29	Warwick . . .	..	..	24	24	71	119
30	Wilts	1	..	2	..	5	8
31	Worcester . .	..	..	1	1	...	2

[1] See above, pp. 54–55.

the frankpledge counties, and prove in a convincing way that there was no lack of frankpledge even in those places which stand low in the table just given. In the pipe rolls one finds a wide geographical distribution within the counties as early as the twelfth century; and the assize rolls reveal not only the same condition in the thirteenth century, but also the maintenance of tithings in the extreme northern parts of the northernmost frankpledge counties.[1] When it is remembered, moreover, that outside of the privileged sections the sheriff not only held the view at regular intervals, but also expected to collect a substantial revenue in so doing, there is every reason for assuming that, except in such unusual cases as have been mentioned, frankpledge suretyship was maintained throughout the thirty counties.

The frankpledge system, although one of the clearest manifestations of strong central government in the England of the twelfth and thirteenth centuries, nevertheless could not escape the influence of that rule of usage which determined all feudal relations: it was not carried into new territory, for the reason that its introduction would have involved an infringement, by the king's sheriffs and justices, of a local freedom from such imposition which constituted a highly prized custom of the county. To compensate for the lack of such a force for the preservation of the peace, thirteenth-century law held the vill responsible for responding to the hue and capturing criminals;[2] but in so large a part of the land was frankpledge suretyship the

---

[1] The eyre roll for Derby, 4 Edward III, mentions the amercement of tithings for the escape of fugitives at Chesterfield and at Hathersage (Public Record Office, Assize Roll, No. 166, m. 25*b*). A similar roll for Stafford, 21 Edward I, (No. 804, mm. 54, 56), shows a similar responsibility in the hundred of Totmonslow, which touches both Cheshire and Derby, and also in vills of the hundred of Seisdon near Shropshire.

[2] See Parker, *Lancashire Assize Rolls* (Record Soc. for Lancashire and Cheshire), i. 88, 106; ii. 280.

established order that both legal compilations and legal enactments could afford to ignore exceptional conditions in the out-
lying districts.   If these districts are left out of the account, the
regular maintenance of the institution in thirty of the counties
and in many of the most populous and prosperous English
municipalities, including London,[1] no less than in small towns
still subject to seigniorial control, is such as to show in practice
a general adherence to the rule that the men of all the vills of
the realm were to be in the suretyship of the tithings.

[1] Hudson (*Leet Jurisdiction in Norwich*, p. lxxi) is in error in assuming
that frankpledge in London meant the providing of only a very few sureties,
sometimes of but two.   In the reference which he cites (*Liber Albus*, ed. Riley, i.
90) frankpledge is used as Bracton uses it for mainpast (cf. Bracton, fol. 124*b*, ii.
306; and Sharpe, *Calendar of the Letterbooks of London*, Book A, p. 216).   The
suretyship of the two pledges had to be given by the stranger within three days
after he came to live in the ward.   View of frankpledge, at which men might be
regularly enrolled, was held but once or twice a year (see *Liber Albus*, i. 38;
Ogle, *Royal Letters to Oxford*, 39–40).

CHAPTER III

ORGANIZATION AND FUNCTIONS OF FRANKPLEDGE

INTEREST in frankpledge suretyship is not due solely to the extraordinary character and wide territorial distribution of the system. Including as it did the greater part of medieval Englishmen, it formed one of the conditions in the environment of the man in humble rank which shaped the social and political sides of his life.

The number of persons in frankpledge may, indeed, as easily be overestimated as the number of counties in which the institution existed. It has been observed that prior to the middle of the twelfth century a legal compiler intimated that even before his day the law in theory required all in the realm to be in tithing;[1] yet it is perfectly clear that this broad assertion, like the requirement in Saxon law that all free men should be in *borh*, went farther than did the rule as it was actually enforced. In other passages the same writer recognizes the fact that some men were not pledged by tithings, but that the host stood pledge for the guest, and, according to a later edition of the work, the man of rank for his household.[2] Although nearly all men were perhaps at one time under obligation to a performance of duty in tithings, yet a considerable and, if conclusions may be drawn from a comparison of twelfth with thirteenth century statements, a constantly growing number were exempt.

[1] *Leges Edw. Conf.*, xx, in Liebermann, *Gesetze*, i. 645; Schmid, *Gesetze*, 502; Thorpe, *Laws*, i. 450.
[2] *Leges Edw. Conf.*, xxi, xxiii, in Liebermann, i. 647, 648.

Even before the *Leges Edwardi* were written a jurist who set forth in the usual sweeping fashion the rule that all free males above the age of twelve should be in frankpledge, immediately proceeded to make an exception by adding that certain classes were required to be in the pledge of their lords,[1] an indication that qualifications to these broad assertions were often perfectly understood even when not expressed. Bracton, who lays down the general principle that every male above twelve, whether free or non-free, ought to be in frankpledge, further increases the list of exceptions;[2] and Britton names still others that were recognized by English law in his day.[3]

The age when a youth must be put in tithing is given as twelve by thirteenth-century writers. Britton, however, who in one passage agrees with Fleta and the *Mirror of Justices* on this point, in another speaks as if fourteen were the age,[4] an impression which has often found its way into works of modern days. This difference in statement is probably due to a difference in local usage; but Britton's earlier assertion, agreeing as it does with Bracton's,[5] gives the law as generally followed in the fifteenth no less than in the thirteenth century.[6] The jurors at the manorial view of frankpledge, as well as those at the sheriff's tourn, presented persons above twelve years of age who were out of tithing.[7] Legal theory on this point seems to have been influenced by the requirement of Canute that all above the age of twelve should take an oath to observe the

---

[1] *Leges Henrici*, viii. 2, 2a, in Liebermann, *Gesetze*, i. 554.

[2] Fol. 124b, ii. 304–306.

[3] Nichols's edition, i. 48–49.

[4] *Ibid.* 48, 181; Fleta, 40, 112; *Mirror of Justices*, 39, 41.

[5] Britton, i. 181.

[6] See *Cart. St. Peter of Gloucester* (Rolls Series), iii. 221; Dugdale, *Monasticon*, ii. 83.

[7] Maitland, *Court Baron*, 68, 71, 72, 97; Young, *Dulwich College*, ii. 281.

peace.[1] This oath, which Bracton says was by the *Leges Edwardi* required in the twelfth century also,[2] was at that time, he seems to assume, made at the view of frankpledge just as it was in his own day.[3] There was, it is true, an argument for excusing such young boys from duty in the tithing on the ground that they obviously could not perform the services required of it; but the rule as to taking the oath seems to have been rigorously enforced both by royal and by manorial officials. Until 1267 persons over twelve years of age appear to have been required to attend the sheriff's tourn; for it was held that, although minors could not make presentments, they ought nevertheless to be present to take oath and to report any felonies which they knew of.[4] After 1267 such persons were still required to attend an inquisition concerning a death.

Only one class of persons above the age of twelve was, according to Bracton, under suretyship of no kind whatever. Men who travelled about so much that they were not to be considered as belonging to one place more than to another could not be put in frankpledge, for this form of security required a residence of a year and a day.[5] Nor could their good behavior be assured by any other kind of pledging; for such a vagrant existence would as a rule so lay them open to suspicion that no man would assume responsibility for them permanently, and no one would be likely to permit them to remain at his home more than two nights, since a third would render him liable for them during their sojourn. The *extraneus transiens* (the *vagabundus* of the fourteenth century) was a person who often fled after committing a crime; but the royal courts always admitted

---

[1] 2 Canute, xxi, in Liebermann, *Gesetze*, i. 324–325.
[2] See also below, p. 130.
[3] Fol. 124b, ii. 306.
[4] Coke, *Second Institute* (1671), 147.
[5] The time from one view of frankpledge to the next.

such itinerancy as excusing a vill for not having a criminal in frankpledge.

All persons except vagrants, then, were, as Bracton held, required either to be in frankpledge or in the mainpast or personal pledge of a responsible person, or else to have some qualification, such as rank, order, or property, which served as surety in place of frankpledge.[1] Such general exceptions to the rule that all males over twelve, both free and serf, should be pledged by tithings may now be considered.

A tacit recognition of the principle that some persons were by their rank and standing excused from finding surety for their observance of the peace was observed under Anglo-Saxon rule in England. Though legislators more than once declared that every freeman must have a *borh* to lead him to justice, certain men were evidently exempt from this requirement,[2] a fact which may be reconciled to the letter of the law by the assumption that, since they were above the grade of ordinary freemen, they were not to be regarded as subject to provisions applicable to that class. A more practical reason for this exemption was, however, that such persons usually had property upon which it was possible to levy in case they became obdurate breakers of the peace. The magnate, or even the small lord with but a few dependents, might through the lands which he held be easily reached in a way that would bring him to terms; but, as has been pointed out, justice could in many cases be had only with great difficulty from the ordinary freeman who was landless, or who had at best but a small amount of property. Hence the necessity that the latter be in *borh*. When in the reign of Henry I frankpledge is found in operation, the same principle holds good. From the reign of William the Conqueror it became necessary for the king to look to the ruling class of Norman

[1] Fol. 124*b*, ii. 306.
[2] See above, p. 19.

magnates to keep in subjection the masses of the vanquished race; and the nobility, already with some jurisdictional powers derived from Saxon days, increased their ability to perform such an office by acquiring feudal justiciary rights from time to time. The Saxon lord had of old been held responsible for the retainers whom he lodged. A later text of the *Leges Edwardi*, which Liebermann dates between 1140 and 1159, shows that archbishops, bishops, earls, and barons were of great importance in maintaining the peace; for they were required to hold both their knights and their household officers and servants in their own pledge, and, if the hue and cry were raised on account of any of these, to punish the offenders in their own courts in case they had grants of "*sake* and *soke* and *toll* and *team* and *infangenethef.*" [1] The magnates themselves, both lay and spiritual, were, according to the medieval conception, custodians of the peace, and hence needed no surety to keep it. If they offended against their suzerain or their vassals, the feudal law of forfeiture afforded a means of punishment which was considered adequate. As to their treatment of peasant dependents no one cared; but the mere fact of their lordship over such persons was assumed to be a sufficient pledge of honorable conduct toward them. They were not expected to be in frankpledge. [2]

The same rule applied to lords in general. The importance of personal lordship in maintaining the public peace has already been traced as far back as the time of Athelstan; and the requirement that the lord act as surety for his own household, firmly fixed in Saxon law by the time of Ethelred, was carried over into Norman days. This arrangement could not, however, be reciprocal like frankpledge, for the dependents of the house-

---

[1] *Leges Edw. Conf.*, xxi, xxi.1, in Liebermann, *Gesetze*, i. 647.
[2] Bracton, fol. 124b, ii. 306.

hold were unable to pledge the good conduct of its head. The lord, therefore, being entirely removed from participation in any system of peace pledge except in the capacity of surety, could himself be brought to accountability only through the agency of the officers of the king or of some other suzerain.

The knights formed another class whose order excused them from frankpledge. Bracton and Britton both recognize this rule as in full force in their day.[1] At an earlier time, about the middle of the twelfth century, it is stated that archbishops, bishops, earls, and barons were required to have their knights in their mainpast to insure order.[2] One may well doubt, however, whether this was true in the thirteenth century, at least when the knights were not connected with a magnate's household establishment; for, according to Britton, their eldest sons, or, as he says in a later and perhaps more corrupt passage, their children, then enjoyed exemption from frankpledge, and nothing more is said of knights in mainpast.[3] Bracton affirms, though in a somewhat vague way, that relatives of knights were exempt. The rule that knights and their eldest sons were excused was certainly enforced, and was so well recognized as to be still in operation in leets at the end of the fifteenth century, after real frankpledge had long since fallen into desuetude.[4]

The clergy also were by virtue of their calling released from any responsibility connected with peace suretyship; for not only was their very order assumed to be sufficient pledge that they would never be guilty of breach of peace, but the performance of such police service as membership in a tithing implied was too palpably of a secular nature to be expected of

---

[1] Bracton, fol. 124b, ii. 304; Britton, i. 48.
[2] *Leges Edw. Conf.*, xxi, in Liebermann, *Gesetze*, i. 647.
[3] Britton, i. 181.
[4] L. T. Smith, *Common-place Book*, 161.

them. Such an exemption is certainly to be understood in the
Saxon legislation requiring all freemen to be in *borh;* and, like
the privilege of the magnate and the lord, it also passed on down
to frankpledge days. Not only was this rule clearly stated in the
legal theory of the thirteenth century,[1] but in actual practice it
was so well recognized when records were first kept that any
man who could succeed in passing himself off even as an itinerant clerk escaped frankpledge duty.[2] In 1292 a student at Cambridge, who had been distrained to a performance of tithing
duty by the lord of the manor in which his home was, recovered
damages in the King's Bench, the court holding that the lord
acted against the law in thus demanding suit of leet from a
clerk.[3] In boroughs, however, clerks who were not clergymen
strictly speaking, and who had families and engaged in business, were sometimes put in frankpledge.[4] In the *Mirror of
Justices* there is even a declaration, but a very doubtful and
contradictory one, that clerks must be in frankpledge.[5]

Besides those whose nobility or order exempted them from
frankpledge, there was a third class whose freehold property
served as security for their observance of the peace. In the
middle of the thirteenth century the rule was that the holding
of a free tenement or of real property in a borough constituted
a surety sufficient to take the place of frankpledge;[6] but this
rule could hardly have been enforced literally, for its observance
would have made frankpledge of very slight importance in
towns in which the typical burgher owned a burgage.

---

[1] Bracton, fol. 124*b*, ii. 304; Britton, i. 48.
[2] Healey, *Somersetshire Pleas*, 58.
[3] *Year Book*, 20–21 Edw. I, 297.
[4] Hudson, *Leet Jurisdiction in Norwich*, p. lxvii.
[5] *Mirror of Justices*, 41; and cf. p. 39, which shows that clerks were exempt
from attending the view of frankpledge.
[6] Bracton, fol. 124*b*, ii. 306.

Whether or not the mere personal status of a freeman was sufficient to excuse him is a question upon which there is room for difference of opinion, but which seems in the main to demand a negative answer. The assize rolls, which regularly declare that a man is not in frankpledge *quia liber*, appear at first sight to show that the itinerant justices recognized such an exemption;[1] but it is very evident that some of these exempt persons could plead other reasons than their free status. The entry concerning a man in Staffordshire who "was not in frankpledge because he was a freeman" has the significant addition that "he held six acres of land freely." Another man, John Sautcheverel, who had no chattels himself but was the son of a knight of the same name who held a large amount of land in Staffordshire and Derbyshire,[2] was thus likely to be excused not only as a freeholder but also as the relative of a knight. Here, then, seems to be good reason for believing that the exemption was made because of a free holding rather than because of a free status. The word freeman may be merely a technical term, just as it was in the sixteenth century. Against making this explanation universal, however, seem to stand the words of Bracton, who in one passage designates among those exempt from frankpledge the magnate, the clerk, the knight and his relatives, the free man, and the like.[3] Yet, as already observed, Bracton fully recognizes the principle that, aside from the classes exempt because of rank, order, property, or similar qualification, the rest of the population both free and

---

[1] Thus Healey, the editor of the rolls published by the Somerset Record Society, considers the words *quia liber* conclusive evidence that only villains were in frankpledge. See his *Somersetshire Pleas*, p. xxx.

[2] Salt Archaeol. Soc., *Collections*, iv. 72 and note, 73 and note.

[3] "Magnates, milites et eorum parentes, clericus, liber homo et hujusmodi" (fol. 124b, ii. 304). Nichols in his edition of Britton (i. 181, note) regards "liber homo" as referring to the military tenant of Norman times; but if this is true "milites" in the passage just quoted is superfluous.

serf must be in tithings. In short, whatever rule is laid down, it must be remembered that the matter of exempting freemen, and the other classes as well, varied with local custom.[1]

It may fairly be assumed, then, that those in frankpledge were not exclusively villains. The development of the system from Saxon *borh*, which was for freemen only, shows very clearly that in the early Norman period, when frankpledge is first mentioned, the general position of the masses could not have been so far depressed as to bring only the unfree into tithing. It appears, indeed, that this depression came about, to a considerable extent, as a result of the writings of Romanizing jurists in the latter half of the twelfth century. Specific mention, in the thirteenth century, of the fact that a man in frankpledge is a villain, when nothing is said as to the status of other men in tithing in the same neighborhood, seems to show that it was not unusual for freemen to be in frankpledge suretyship. Even in the early fourteenth century such persons were still sometimes in tithing. This had been the case in the hamlet of "Huncyndon" in Derbyshire, where the tenants had been *libere tenentes* and not *nativi;* but by 1324 such tenants were no longer there.[2] Although at Dudley in Worcestershire a man was not in tithing in 1274 *quia liber de burgo*,[3] yet at Norwich about 1315, in spite of Bracton's assertion that the possession of real property in a city was sufficient surety in itself, free burghers were undoubtedly in frankpledge.[4] In the city of Canterbury freemen might also be in frankpledge.[5] In London the ordi-

---

[1] "Secundum consuetudinem patriae" (Bracton, ii. 304). That this expression refers to local custom is conclusively shown by its repetition, a few lines farther on, in relation to a practice in but one county.

[2] Salt Archaeol. Soc., *Collections*, v. pt. i. 87–88. See above, p. 64, note 1.

[3] Public Record Office, Assize Roll, No. 1026, m. 38.

[4] Hudson, *Leet Jurisdiction in Norwich*, p. lvi.

[5] *Rot. Hundred.*, i. 203.

nances of the lorimer's gild forbade the receiving of any stranger, whether master or journeyman, until he was in frankpledge;[1] and in Leicester as late as 1376 some three hundred men were in frankpledge, including workmen, masters, and servants.[2] It by no means appears, moreover, that the royal assent, in 1293, to the famous customs of Kent, which declared that "all the bodies of Kentishmen be free,"[3] destroyed frankpledge in that county. The adherence to these customs at a slightly earlier period certainly had no such effect. In the early fourteenth century, however, to be in a rural tithing in East England was synonymous with being in villainage;[4] yet in 1329 a freeman on an Essex manor is mentioned as being in frankpledge.[5] These few facts will perhaps point to the conclusion that the boroughs longest retained frankpledge as a general police measure; while in the country districts, after the thirteenth century, the man who held his land by a free tenure usually had property interests extensive enough to assure an ample court payment through confiscation in case he became a fugitive from justice. Frankpledge was unquestionably an institution that chiefly affected villains;[6] but to affirm that the freeman as such was released from frankpledge obligations is clearly incorrect.

Persons either physically or mentally unable to perform such duties as frankpledge imposed were not held responsible for their discharge. About 1290 a London writer says that deaf mutes, sick folk, idiots, and lepers were exempt.[7] There certainly

---

[1] *Liber Custumarum* (ed. Riley), pt. i. 79.
[2] Bateson, *Records of Leicester*, ii. 153.
[3] *Statutes of the Realm*, i. 223.
[4] Hudson, *Leet Jurisdiction in Norwich*, p. lxviii.
[5] Clark, in *Eng. Hist. Review*, xix. 716.
[6] See Vinogradoff, *Villainage*, 66.
[7] *Mirror of Justices*, 39.

was nowhere any attempt to put lepers in tithings, for it was the duty of the jurors in the local police jurisdictions promptly to present the names of such persons that they might be segregated;[1] and it is equally clear that English law in this period recognized the disabilities both of the idiot and of the lunatic, and gave suitable excuses to those infirm in body. As for deaf mutes one cannot be so sure; but in rural districts they were perhaps so few in number that the question would not often arise.

Besides those who were not required to be members of tithings because of rank, order, property, or disability, there was one other class of the population not generally in frankpledge, — those, namely, who were in the mainpast or personal pledge of some one individual. The law of mainpast can in its essential features easily be traced back through the laws of Canute and Ethelred, which held the lord responsible for the men of his household, to the law of Edmund requiring every man to pledge the good conduct of those whom he maintained and lodged, and ultimately to the Kentish law of the late seventh century, which made the host a similar pledge for the stranger whom he received for more than three nights. These provisions, with some new details, were carried over bodily by the law books of the twelfth century.[2] Bracton makes a man's mainpast consist, first, of his *folgheres* ("followers"), who, if accused of any charge while in his service, can be legally dismissed by him only after they are purged of crime; and, secondly, of the household which he supplies with food and clothing, or which he virtually supplies with food through wages, such as the domestics or the servingmen and hirelings of his family. To these he also adds persons entertained in the house, following

---

[1] Maitland, *Court Baron*, 134.

[2] *Leges Henrici*, viii. 2–5, xli. 7–8, lxvi. 7, in Liebermann, *Gesetze*, i. 554, 568, 586; *Leis Willelme*, lii, and Pseudo-Ingulf version, xlviii, *ibid.* 519; *Leges Edw. Conf.*, xxi, xxiii, *ibid.* 647, 648. See above, pp. 16, 20.

the old Anglo-Saxon rule, brought over into Norman times, which held that the first night the traveller was to be regarded as a stranger, the second night as a guest, the third as a member of the household.[1] Finally, he says that any man might receive another into his mainpast if the other so desired, but that, pending investigation of an accusation against the person received, neither the surety nor the one pledged was to withdraw from the arrangement after it was once made any more than one might withdraw from his tithing.[2] It will be remembered that Bracton calls this manner of pledging *francum plegium alicuius*, in opposition to *decenna* or tithing suretyship.

The word mainpast (*manupastus*) is but a Latin version of the Anglo-Saxon *hlafeatan*, loaf-eaters. In the strict sense of the term, then, the mainpast of the head of a household are "those whom his hand feeds," [3] — not only servants and retainers, but all other members of his household as well. There seems to be every reason for thinking, however, that the law of mainpast as stated by Bracton is substantially the same as that followed prior to the Norman Conquest. Evidences of a tendency to consider the members of the family under this form of suretyship appear at a comparatively late date. The son is sometimes found to be in the mainpast of his father,[4] or the younger brother in that of the older; [5] but it seems to be only when the father or the brother is a man of standing, for in one case a father is fined for failure to have his son put in frankpledge.[6] The close analogy which Bracton draws between the

---

[1] *Leges Henrici*, viii. 5, and *Leges Edw. Conf.*, xxiii, in Liebermann, *Gesetze*, i. 554, 648.

[2] Bracton, fol. 124b, ii. 306–309. See also Britton, i. 49.

[3] Pollock and Maitland, *English Law* (1895), i. 555.

[4] As in Healey, *Somersetshire Pleas*, 248 (A. D. 1243).

[5] Maitland, *Pleas of the Crown for Gloucester*, No. 101.

[6] Maitland, *Court Baron*, 72.

two kinds of pledging seems to indicate that no householder would be held responsible for pledging any one who was too young to be put in frankpledge, but that responsibility in the two systems began at the same age.

The theory that women were to be considered in mainpast is presented only at the end of the thirteenth century, and then apparently to explain the fact that they never had been, and obviously never could be, put in tithings.[1] Britton regarded the exemption of women as universal, assigning as a reason for the law that a woman could not be outlawed the fact that she could not be appointed to any tithing.[2] Earlier writers had tacitly taken this exception for granted; Britton accounted for it on the assumption that women were in the mainpast of some male relative.[3] It is evident, however, that this theory was not strictly applied by the courts. In 1302 one woman, probably a widow of some property, was so far free from the tutelage of any male relative that she was recognized as holding in her own mainpast a son whom she was bringing up at home.[4] Even when a woman criminal was waived,[5] it does not appear that any individual was fined for failure to produce her in court.

As already observed, clerics were not expected to be under suretyship. In the time of Henry II the head of a religious order is mentioned as holding the members in his mainpast: grants to the abbey of St. George of Bocherville in Normandy and to

---

[1] The *Mirror of Justices* says in one passage (ch. xvii, pp. 39, 41) that women are not exempt; but in view of the well-known inaccuracy of the work this assertion seems to have been made for purposes of euphony, and may have been influenced by the fact that women were often in attendance at the view of frankpledge. The entry "non fuit in decenna quia mulier" is of frequent occurrence in assize rolls for the time of Edward I.

[2] Britton, i. 50, 181.

[3] *Ibid.* 49.

[4] *Year Book*, 30–31 Edw. I, 203.

[5] A woman could not be outlawed.

three abbeys in England are made in each case "to the abbot and his mainpast." [1] These entries probably refer to mainpast merely in the sense of a household, with no idea that the abbot was responsible for producing his monks in court; but in the thirteenth century priors and abbots were regularly amerced for not producing men of their mainpast. [2]

Of the members of the household who were in mainpast, those not of the family were far the more likely to need suretyship. It is these persons to whom the attention of law-writers and law-makers is chiefly directed, and it is likewise this class in mainpast which appears oftenest in the records of criminal courts. The requirement that strangers were to be regarded as in the suretyship of the head of the house in which they were received for three nights or more shows that they were looked upon with real suspicion. There was, indeed, a great deal of crime committed by vagrants who were not in suretyship of any kind. If, therefore, such persons became members of a community it was very essential that they be under some sort of pledge; and from as far back as there is any written English law mainpast had been the form provided for them. Before they could be compelled to enroll in a tithing they had to be in residence in the community a year and a day. In 1166 Henry II deemed it essential for the maintenance of the public peace strictly to reiterate for towns and boroughs the old law requiring those who received such strangers in house or on land to take them *in manu* to have them before the justices if required. [3] Ten years later he made more stringent still the conditions under which travellers might be received, by requiring that no one, in either borough or vill, should entertain a stranger in his house for

---

[1] Dugdale, *Monasticon*, vi. pt. ii. 1067.

[2] Salt Archaeol. Soc., *Collections*, iv. 211, 214.

[3] Assize of Clarendon, ch. x, in Stubbs, *Select Charters*, 144.

more than one night without reasonable excuse, unless he were willing to have the person in court. Furthermore, when the traveller left it must be by day and in the presence of the · neighbors.[1] More than a century later, according to Britton, it was the duty of the jury at the view of frankpledge to present not only the names of persons above the age of twelve and not of the exempt classes who were out of tithing, but also the names of their receivers and of those who had them in mainpast, as well as "of vagrants through the country who are not of any one's mainpast, and are of suspicious character."[2] The writer of the *Mirror of Justices* would excuse from frankpledge only foreigners who are "messengers, pilgrims, or merchants,"[3] a fact which shows a disposition to grant no indulgence to vagrants.

The greater part of those in mainpast who were likely to be troublesome were, however, domestics and persons serving in a household for wages. Although Bracton elsewhere lays down the rule of responsibility for all whom a man receives into his house or whom by special arrangement he takes into his mainpast, yet he carefully repeats the old provision in the later edition of the *Leges Edwardi*, that episcopal and lay magnates, to whom he adds persons with regalian liberties, shall be responsible for leading to justice not only their knights, but also their squires and servants, such as stewards, butlers, chamberlains, cooks, and bakers.[4] If these are not produced when required, their master must pay a forfeit. The words that follow, "so shall it be observed concerning all who are of any one's mainpast," show the care taken by the writer to make it clear that such responsibility was fixed on the heads of both great and

---

[1] Assize of Northampton, ch. ii, in Stubbs, *Select Charters*, 151.

[2] Britton, i. 181.

[3] *Mirror*, 41. Those "in ward" are also exempted here; but ward is only the name for frankpledge in cities and towns of importance.

[4] Fol. 124*b*, ii. 306. Fleta (p. 40) also repeats this law.

small households. To this general law of mainpast there might, however, as Bracton goes on to show, be some modification according to local custom. In 1221, for example, a justice in eyre had recognized a rule in the county of Hertford according to which no man was responsible for a default on the part of his mainpast unless subsequently to the latter's felony or flight he had received him again into his house;[1] but this rule was an exception to the general practice in other counties at about the same time,[2] as well as both earlier[3] and later. Some idea of the exact strictness with which the law of mainpast was ordinarily enforced may be gained from the case of a certain Roger Barel, a resident of the county of Somerset, who in 1243 was declared "at mercy" by the justices in eyre for not producing one Nicholas; a man in his mainpast, who had fled after burning Roger's own house.[4]

Bearing in mind exemptions made on account of rank, order, property, disability, or connection with a responsible householder, one may say that persons of all other classes were in frankpledge. These constituted the great body of Englishmen below the rank of nobility or of knighthood who were neither clerks nor freeholders. To be exact, however, it is necessary to include in tithing part of the mainpast class; for persons in mainpast in one place might be in frankpledge elsewhere. Thus, in some boroughs the close connection of the servant class with the town industries led to their inclusion in its general system of police suretyship.[5] Ordinarily this would happen also when strangers

---

[1] Bracton, ii. 304. According to one manuscript it was in Hereford.

[2] See, for example, Maitland, *Pleas of the Crown for Gloucester*, No. 185; Salt Archaeol. Soc., *Collections*, iv. 214.

[3] *Pipe Rolls*, 12 Hen. II, 66 (Rutland), and 21 Hen. II, 194 (Hants).

[4] Healey, *Somersetshire Pleas*, 299.

[5] Hudson, *Leet Jurisdiction in Norwich*, p. lxvi; Bateson, *Records of Leicester*, ii. 153.

or temporary sojourners were received in mainpast; for their tithing membership at home was likely to be retained, though doubtless often unknown to those who temporarily acted as their pledges. A resident of another county was apparently not put in tithing when he was known to live elsewhere;[1] in London the principle was distinctly enunciated that a man could have responsibility to but one tithing at a time.[2] Nor was one required to be in a tithing if one was in ward in a borough, for the two situations amounted to the same thing. A temporary sojourner was pledged only by coming into some one's mainpast. In cases in which both mainpast and frankpledge arrangements were effected in places near enough together to be within reach of the same itinerant justices, a head of a household to which a man joined himself was sometimes amerced on his account, and the vill where he was, or should have been, in frankpledge was likewise amerced for the same default.[3] Outside the boroughs mainpast and frankpledge were in general mutually exclusive; hence these exceptional cases, being confined to travellers, were comparatively rare.

That a large part of the population of England south of the Trent and east of Hereford and Shropshire was in tithing there can be little doubt. Aside from the exemptions mentioned by writers of the thirteenth century, practically all of the villains were held subject to the obligations and duties of frankpledge. There seems to be some reason for supposing that in the time of Edward I this class of peasants comprised two-thirds of the whole English population;[4] but it is to be remembered that the system also embraced some rural freemen, and that it was en-

---

[1] Healey, *Somersetshire Pleas*, 255, 272.

[2] *Mirror of Justices*, 39; also p. 41, where it is said that those in ward are exempt from any other tithing duty.

[3] Healey, *Somersetshire Pleas*, 269.

[4] Cheyney, in *Eng. Hist. Review*, xv. 20.

forced in many boroughs, including the most populous English communities, where servitude did not exist. Moreover, although it would appear that in general only villains were in frankpledge at the beginning of the fourteenth century, this was probably not true at an earlier time. At any rate, the law as stated by Bracton would have required the putting in frankpledge of many rural freemen without property enough to serve as surety for their good behavior. If one accepts the most extreme assertion that it is possible to find in Bracton, and understands it as exempting all freemen, one must still bear in mind that even this rule was varied by local usage,[1] that in some rural as well as urban communities men of free status were undoubtedly in frankpledge, and that travellers who were in frankpledge at home could hardly have been villains.[2]

The frankpledge unit, the tithing, which claimed a part in the activities of so many persons, is variously designated in the records under the names *decenna, francplegium, fridborg, tedinga,* and *thething a,* but after the twelfth century usually as *decenna* or *tedinga.* In the southeast, especially in Kent, it is called a *borg* or *borgha;*[3] in the pipe rolls of Henry II for Berkshire occurs one reference to the institution under the name of *borgus.*[4]

The number of men in a frankpledge tithing undoubtedly tended to increase between the beginning of the twelfth and the end of the thirteenth century, for the theoretical number is greater in the reign of Edward I than in that of Henry I. The old traditional number in a tithing was ten, a good round figure probably borrowed by the early Norman practice from the Saxon tithing of Canute, but in any event to be found even

---

[1] See above, p. 77.

[2] Healey, *Somersetshire Pleas,* 272.

[3] "Nec fuit in Borgha quia extraneus ": Public Record Office, Assize Roll, No. 376, m. 2b.

[4] *Pipe Roll,* 23 Hen. II, 49.

earlier in the London *frithgild* tithing of Athelstan's time. So strong was this tradition that prior to the thirteenth century it had fixed upon the tithing and the tithingman respectively the names *decenna* and *decennarius*, by which they were to be known permanently in law Latin, and had in some cases caused the frankpledge system to be designated as "decennial suretyship" (*fideiussio decennalis*) and the tithing as a *decimatio*.[1] All this seems to indicate that the Saxon tithing included ten at least, and that in the time of Henry I there was an effort to maintain the frankpledge tithing at that number as a minimum. To keep the tithing intact was one of the objects of the two special hundred courts held yearly at the later period.[2]

The fact that the frankpledge population of a whole vill or manor often constituted a tithing shows that, although ten was probably the minimum, the actual number of members must have varied considerably. The requirement of the Magna Carta of 1217, and of subsequent reissues, that "the tithing be kept entire as was wont,"[3] seems to have been designed to maintain a minimum size of tithing no less than to keep up the tithing organization. Before the last of the reissues by Edward I the tithing appears to have contained more than ten. In the thirteenth century it was sometimes, especially by the jurists who wrote in French during the reign of Edward I, called a dozen (*douzaine, duodena*) and its members dozeners,[4] a group-

---

[1] *Leges Edw. Conf.*, xx. 1, in Liebermann, *Gesetze*, i. 645; Liebermann, *Consiliatio Cnuti*, 13.

[2] *Leges Henrici*, viii. 1, in Liebermann, *Gesetze*, i. 554; Schmid, *Gesetze*, 441.

[3] Magna Carta of 1217, ch. xlii, *Statutes of the Realm*, i. 17–19; reissues of 1225 and 1245, *ibid.* 24, 31; reissue of 1297, ch. xxv, *ibid.* 118.

[4] See Liebermann, *Ueber die Leges Edw. Conf.*, 30 (note 9), 78; Vinogradoff, *Villainage*, 363, note 4; Britton, i. 48; *Mirror of Justices*, 39, where *dozeine* and *diseine* are the forms used. Maitland shows that the statement of the *Leges Edwardi*, ch. xx, is against the assumption that a tithing has always been a tenth of a long hundred. He suggests (*Select Pleas in Manorial Courts*, p. xxix,

ing by twelves which, as already observed,[1] was probably due to a revival of Saxon precedents.

The early thirteenth-century assertion that a tithing contained ten, twenty, or thirty according to local custom,[2] shows a diversity in practice made necessary by the fact that in Kent and the shires of the old West Saxon kingdom the prevailing usage was for the men of a whole township or district to form a single tithing.[3] In these parts of England the number in tithing thus usually depended on the number of residents of the class that was subject to the frankpledge obligation. In the boroughs where frankpledge existed, the tithings, or the wards that sometimes served in their places, were groups also founded on territorial divisions.[4] Though the personal basis of the tithing continued to be maintained in most places, yet there are tithing-lists of both town and country which show, instead of the capital pledge with the traditional nine other pledges, a capital pledge with sometimes from twenty to twenty-five others.[5] In tithing-lists of the fourteenth century there seems to be no change in numbers on account of either increase or decrease in population. One tithing was not incorporated with others as soon as it numbered less than twelve or even less than ten. About the beginning of the fifteenth century one rural place had on its tithing-lists capital pledges with eight or nine, or even with two

note 4) that the word which Bracton writes *dozeine* is formed from the Latin *decena* by the intermediation of such a form as *deciona;* but this etymological change could hardly have altered the plain reading of the law without the precedent in Anglo-Saxon custom that has been suggested elsewhere in this study.

[1] See above, pp. 21, 28–29.

[2] A gloss on the Holkham MSS. (Liebermann, *Consiliatio Cnuti*, 13). This corrects Palgrave's version (*Commonwealth*, ii. p. cxxv, note 34), which is obviously wrong in giving the number of members as ten, seventy, or eighty.

[3] Healey, *Somersetshire Pleas*, p. xxx.

[4] Bateson, *Records of Leicester*, i. pp. xlix, 365; Kitchin, *Charter to St. Giles Fair*, 34.

[5] Hudson, *Leet Jurisdiction in Norwich*, p. l.

or three, associates; and as these died or moved away or gained exemption from frankpledge their names were crossed out, till the capital pledge sometimes stood alone on the list.[1] Such a condition, however, so clearly indicates the decadence of frankpledge that one is hardly justified in assuming its existence at a much earlier time. In an Essex tithing in 1428 there were still fourteen pledges besides the two capital ones.[2]

In referring officially to a tithing different modes of designation were followed. In rare cases the group was mentioned as the tithing of such or such a fugitive member;[3] but ordinarily two other forms of reference were used. As early as the reign of Henry II the tithing either was named for its head man, or else, if there was but one frankpledge association for a vill or district, it bore the name of that district. Thus one of the earliest frankpledge entries in the pipe rolls mentions "the tithing of Ralph Smith,"[4] a form usually, though not always, followed in the east and midlands and sometimes in the west and south. Reference to "the tithing of Lasham" in Hampshire at a little later period shows the form of nomenclature used more or less in the regions where the territorial tithing still existed,[5] — namely, in the counties south of the Thames, in the county of Gloucester, and less frequently in the counties of Warwick, Worcester, and Stafford.[6] Its use elsewhere seems to have been due to the fact that a vill was small and had but one personal tithing, rather

---

[1] Harston in Cambridgeshire. See Appendix C, below.

[2] Young, *Dulwich College*, ii. 285.

[3] *Pipe Roll*, 16 Hen. II, 148, 149; *Rot. Cur. Regis* (ed. Palgrave), i. 203, 207; Turner, *Select Pleas of the Forest*, 1.

[4] *Pipe Roll*, 12 Hen. II, 129 (Essex and Hereford).

[5] *Ibid.* 21 Hen. II, 194.

[6] "Tithing of Esse of the Prior of Tanton" (Healey, *Somersetshire Pleas*, 23); "tithing of the Hospital of Perton" (*ibid.* 298). It is sometimes considered necessary to give the name of the tithingman in addition to that of the place. See, for example, *ibid.* 46, 50, 272.

than to any general policy of making tithings follow territorial
lines.   In other words, "tithing" was in the south and west a
designation for a district and also for the frankpledge organization of its inhabitants; whereas in the other frankpledge counties
the vill was the district, and the tithing its inhabitants of a given
frankpledge group.[1]

The duties of the frankpledge tithing may be classified under
three heads, — those resulting from its *borh* character, those
springing from its nature considered purely as a tithing, and
those incidental to its general relation to the police jurisdiction.
These duties were discharged under the direction of a capital
pledge, who in many cases came to represent the whole tithing.
For refusal of due obedience to him, especially in the matter
of financial contribution, a tithing was subject to amercement.[2]

Like the Saxon *borh*, the frankpledge *friborg* was a pledge for
the appearance of its members in court.   Though this pledging
was technical and compulsory, it was spoken of in the same
language as the obligation of the mainpernor who of his own
will bailed a man out of custody and became surety for his
appearance at the proper time.   According to the records subsequent to 1166, if the individual escaped, or for any other
reason was not produced when he should be, his pledge, whether
an individual or a tithing, was subject to amercement by the
justices in eyre "for not having the person who was pledged."[3]

---

[1] See Palgrave, *Commonwealth*, i. 198.   Healey (*Somersetshire Pleas*, p. xxx)
holds that the word tithing in the shires of old Wessex had no territorial signifi-
cation when used with reference to frankpledge; but since, as he himself shows,
the frankpledge tithing included the men of the territorial tithing, it seems correct to say that the former was territorial as well as personal.

[2] Maitland, *Select Pleas in Manorial Courts*, 169; Dugdale, *Monasticon*,
ii. 83.

[3] See, for example, Salt Archaeol. Soc., *Collections*, i. 78; also *Pipe Roll*,
22 Hen. II, 167.   Cf. Healey, *Somersetshire Pleas*, 98–101 (A. D. 1225); also
Maitland, *Pleas of the Crown for Gloucester*, Nos. 118–119, 123–125, 130–133.

The theory of the law held by the writer of the *Leges Edwardi* was that the tithing which failed to produce an accused member was not only liable to a fine for default of this duty, but was also responsible for making good whatever damage he had done, unless the head man and two other members could establish the tithing's innocence of complicity in the crime and flight by their own oath and that of nine others (the capital pledge and the two leading men of each of three neighboring tithings).[1] This probably never was an actual legal rule, certainly not later than the early twelfth century. After 1166, the date at which these matters begin to be systematically recorded, the accusation against a tithing in such a case is no longer subjected to the compurgatory process, but is tendered by a regular presentment jury of twelve. The direct liability of a tithing in the matter of a flight appears only in its amercement for failure to produce delinquent members.

In the event of flight for a crime, the question to what tithing the criminal belonged became one of the points of inquest touching the case, in order that liability for his flight might be fixed. In the thirteenth century the coroner was required to look into this question carefully when holding the customary inquest of his office in the investigation of violent deaths, and to report to the justices, among other matters, to what tithing a fugitive criminal belonged, or, if the man was not in frankpledge but was of the class that should be thus pledged, in what vill he had been received. In the former case, even though the fugitive was taken by others and brought to prison, his tithing was fined for not producing him unless it bailed him from prison and presented him at the proper time. In the latter case the vill was amerced for receiving a man out of frankpledge.[2]

---

[1] *Leges Edw. Conf.*, xx. 3, in Liebermann, *Gesetze*, i. 646. See Pollock and Maitland, *English Law* (1895), ii. 530, note.

[2] Bracton, fol. 124*b*, ii. 304.

The amount paid by the surety in cases of escape was, according to Anglo-Saxon law and the twelfth-century *leges*, at least equivalent to the *wergeld* of the fugitive.[1] In actual practice, from the time of Henry II to that of Edward I the amount exacted from the pledge of an escaped criminal was usually half a mark, whether the suretyship was that of the lord for his mainpast, the tithing for its member, or the mainpernor for the person bailed from custody. Larger sums were occasionally paid, especially when the suretyship was of the last-named variety (which was often employed), or when the offender was a man of rank or standing. When the justices in eyre first undertook the systematic enforcement of the frankpledge obligation in 1166 they collected thirty shillings, two marks, or even forty shillings.[2] Such sums were sometimes exacted at a later time; but by 1175 it seems to have been the rule to demand half a mark as the price of an evasion of justice by a man of the frankpledge or the mainpast class.[3] This mitigation of the severity of the law apparently came as the result of a deliberate policy to make exactions upon men of the lower classes proportionate to their ability to pay, for it is paralleled in the collection of the murder fine from the hundred.[4] If a suspect fled from fear and his innocence was established, he was allowed to return; but it does not appear that the amercement of the tithing for his flight was remitted. The liability was just the

---

[1] *Leges Henrici*, viii. 2, xli. 8, in Liebermann, *Gesetze*, i. 554, 568; *Leis Willelme*, iii. 1, 2, 5, *ibid.* 495–496.

[2] *Pipe Roll*, 12 Hen. II, 108.

[3] See, for example, *ibid.* 22 Hen. II, 167. Cf. Healey, *Somersetshire Pleas*, 98–101, 234; Maitland, *Pleas of the Crown for Gloucester*, Nos. 118–119, 130–133; *Gesta Abbat. Monast. S. Albani* (Rolls Series), iii. 63–64.

[4] According to the writers of the early twelfth century, this fine, when first demanded by the Norman kings, was forty-six marks; but the pipe roll of the thirty-first year of Henry I, and similar rolls of Henry II, show that only four, five, or six marks were usually collected.

same when the culprit found sanctuary and abjured the realm.
Even if he was captured by others and delivered to prison,
the tithing was still amerciable because it had not itself captured and produced him.[1]

Obligation to produce at trial involved not only the paying
for the escape of men in tithing but also the custody of captured
criminals till the next session of the trial court. In those days,
when the castles were the prisons, the cost of imprisonment was
usually to be met by the prisoner; moreover, since such a source
of income as exactions upon this pretext afforded was not to be
overlooked by bailiffs of castles, an amount was often charged
for putting a man under bail. For imprisoning men of the
peasant class, however, who were unable to make such payments, there was not the same motive. In such cases, unless
the offence were particularly heinous, the man's tithing was
charged with his custody after he had been brought before the
keeper of a prison or some other official.[2] As late as 1340 the
tithing performed an analogous function in manorial affairs
by taking into custody, until an accounting was rendered, the
manorial reeve who had ill tithed the goods of the lord to the
damage of the rector.[3] The justices in eyre followed the rule
that, if a man had been attached by his own tithing and did not
appear in court, his tithing associates were responsible and
were to be amerced. In 1221 it is recorded that a man taken
on the appeal of an approver of Bristol was committed to the tithing of the vill of Tetbury.[4] On the lands of the prior of Brooke
in Kent the *borhsealdor* and his *borg* were required to lead
to the hundred of Wye any *extraneus* thief attached, as well

[1] Healey, *Somersetshire Pleas*, 260–262; Bracton, fol. 124*b*, ii. 304.
[2] Healey, *Somersetshire Pleas*, 37; Maitland, *Pleas of the Crown for Gloucester*, No. 241.
[3] Maitland, *Court Baron*, 105.
[4] Maitland, *Pleas of the Crown for Gloucester*, No. 227.

as any man of the tenement of Brooke who was arrested for theft.[1]

The necessity of guarding a neighbor apprehended for crime, who was likely to escape at any time and subject his custodians to a fine, was bad enough, and the obligation of making the journey with him to the hundred or the county court added materially to the burden; but, worse still, a tithing might be required to produce an erring member before the court at Westminster. At the Trinity term of the *coram rege* court in 1220 a man appealed of robbery by an approver at Windsor was committed to the custody of Peter Miller of Eton and his tithing "to have at summons." [2] But Windsor was no great distance from London; and the tithing near by was probably made up of men of the royal domain who would be accounted for on their journeys to London by royal officials, as may have been the case with Peter Miller, the head man. The performance of such police duty by a tithing of poor rustics in a community farther away would, however, doubtless have been impossible; for a tithing consisting mainly of serfs must have offered too many chances for their escape from the manor.

The custody obligation of the tithing, as just shown by the case of the *extraneus* thief, might be assumed when the person replevied was not one of the associates of the group. The tithing might also, like any individual, bail a man from prison,[3] such action being theoretically voluntary on its part. A man in one tithing was sometimes thus bailed by another tithing in conjunction with his own; [4] and occasionally a man guilty of homicide who sought sanctuary came from the church into

---

[1] Scargill-Bird, *Custumals of Battle Abbey* (Camden Soc.), 136.
[2] *Bracton's Note Book*, iii. 379.
[3] Maitland, *Pleas of the Crown for Gloucester*, No. 269.
[4] *Ibid.* No. 264.

the custody of two tithings.[1] In an age when the sheriff or over-lord was given to the exaction of considerable sums of money from the tithing on various illegal pretexts, there must have been frequent temptation to burden it with the custody of accused criminals on the assumption that such obligation was voluntarily assumed. In 1221, for example, a man guilty of causing a death was committed by precept of the justices to a Gloucestershire tithing for the payment of one mark, an amount which in some cases could hardly have failed to be a consideration for putting a man in charge of a tithing to which he had never belonged. Moreover, it was not always possible to incarcerate a criminal in a castle in the regular way. During the Barons' War, following the death of John, William Marshal the regent had such need of the fortifications at Gloucester Castle that he would permit no one to be imprisoned there. For this reason a man accused of homicide was committed to a tithing to be had before the justices; but in extenuation of this proceeding it is recorded that no one spoke against the accused.[2] Sometimes the townsmen themselves prevented the incarceration of a prisoner in their castle, and so left the tithing still responsible.[3]

When police duty was wrongfully laid upon a tithing, its members, who were of lowly station, could hardly risk withstanding the great personage, perhaps a royal favorite, who demanded it. In the hundred rolls there is a complaint that the prior of Christ Church, Canterbury, took of the *borg* of Adisham four pounds for the escape of a certain robber, and that the justices in eyre further amerced the *borg* a hundred shillings for the same default of duty; likewise that the same prior took of the *borg* of " La Leye "[4] a hundred shillings under similar

---

[1] Maitland, *Pleas of the Crown for Gloucester*, No. 315.
[2] *Ibid.* No. 419.   [3] *Rot. Hundred.*, i. 181.   [4] The modern Leigh?

circumstances, although the case was one which belonged to the king alone, and that the royal bailiff of the same *borg* collected three shillings more on the same score.[1] At an earlier time the notorious Engelard de Cigony exacted a hundred shillings from the tithing of the vill of Tetbury in Gloucestershire for the escape of an accused criminal who had been committed to its custody.[2]

The great increase in the number of duties of the *borh* tithing as early as 1220 did not diminish the number of those which it performed as a tithing proper. Just as the Saxon tithing of Edgar pursued and captured thieves, so the frankpledge tithing, at least from the time of Henry I, acted in a similar capacity. Even if one of the associates of the Saxon *borh* committed a crime, the others who were responsible for his appearance at trial had to capture him and take him into custody or else pay a fine. When the *borh* and the tithing were consolidated in frank-pledge, the tithing not only continued to make arrests in such cases, but retained its former general police competence as well, as may be gathered from what has been said in regard to the custody obligation of the tithing; for in the ordinary course of events the criminal would naturally be handed over to the tithing that arrested him. But more substantial proofs on this point are not wanting. The pipe rolls of Henry II and his two sons show clearly enough that the tithing made arrests; but whether or not it apprehended persons other than its own members is a question to which the extreme brevity of these records gives no direct answer. It is significant, however, that, as soon as court records are sufficiently explicit to afford any definite information, one finds the tithing, like its Anglo-Saxon proto-type, making arrests in all sorts of cases, raising the hue and

---

[1] *Rot. Hundred.*, i. 205.
[2] Maitland, *Pleas of the Crown for Gloucester*, No. 227.

cry,[1] and pursuing the offender in force. When the hue was raised anywhere in a vill, all its residents, whether in frankpledge or not, were expected to join in the pursuit. Thus it frequently happened throughout England that a whole vill was fined for failure to do its duty in such cases,[2] or that a tithing was assisted in taking a criminal by other residents of the vill.[3]

As a rule, in the Gloucester pleas of 1221 the tithing is found making arrests which a peace officer would ordinarily be expected to make.[4] Moreover, the finders of a dead body, and in some cases the witnesses of a violent or an accidental death, — persons who were presumed to be under suspicion of causing such death until their innocence was established in case they did not voluntarily appear, — were in various instances attached and brought to the inquest by a tithing sent for that purpose,[5] probably at the direction of the coroner. To secure the appearance in court of an important witness, a tithing might be charged with the duty of bringing before the justices a person who had raised the hue.[6] When five brothers of the well-known Basset family were appealed for causing the death of a neighbor, two tithings were sent to take them, and clearly by order of the sheriff or the justices, for the case had already been settled between the Bassets and the widow of the deceased.[7] An instance in which the justices gave orders for custody by a tithing has already been noticed.[8] This activity of the tithing

[1] Maitland, *Select Pleas of the Crown*, No. 36 (Lincolnshire eyre, A. D. 1202).
[2] As, for example, in Maitland's *Pleas of the Crown for Gloucester*, p. 126.
[3] *Ibid.* No. 404.
[4] *Ibid.* Nos. 21, 280. Page 119 of Maitland's work shows that the former of these territorial tithings actually served as a frankpledge tithing as well.
[5] *Ibid.* Nos. 84, 135, 153, 221, 280, 282, 444; Maitland, *Select Pleas of the Crown*, Nos. 108, 127.
[6] Maitland, *Pleas of the Crown for Gloucester*, No. 383.
[7] *Ibid.* No. 101, and note.
[8] Above, p. 93.

7

under the eyes of royal peace officers who directed its move-
ments seems to be another feature which links it to the tithing
of Edgar under the control of the hundredman. In fact, the
frankpledge tithing is to be found under the supervision of the
royal bailiff also, at one time attending him when he is making
an arrest,[1] at another mulcted by him for dereliction of duty.[2]
By a charter of Edward III to St. Giles Fair, Winchester, in
1349, tithingmen and tithings were put under the direction
of aldermen for the attaching of transgressors against the law
and customs of the fair.[3]

Subordination to the local peace authorities, and frequent
attendance at criminal trials, brought upon the tithing a third
set of duties of a police nature which were distinct from any
known to have belonged to either the Saxon *borh* or the Saxon
tithing. These duties were especially prominent in the south
of England, where the tithings, following territorial lines as
they did, were likely to be numerically greater than elsewhere,
and to include most of the men of a given community who would
be present on such occasions. A tithing also, whether willingly
or not, often performed functions connected with medieval
English justice which were usually or occasionally executed by
a number of individuals, the community in this way assuming
corporate liability in place of the joint obligation of a few individuals. This was true in the south of England particularly.
Under the general summons to the eyre, the various tithings
seem to have been expected to appear before the justices to
assist in making presentments of crimes or to give testimony in
trials of offences, as well as to lead to trial criminals under their
custody. A special privilege enjoyed by the men of Kent and

---

[1] Healey, *Somersetshire Pleas*, 30.

[2] *Rot. Hundred.*, i. 205.

[3] Kitchin, *Charter to St. Giles Fair*, 34. In this case the aldermen were
officers of the bishop.

recorded before the justices in 1293 was a provision exempting gavelkinders from responding generally to this summons and permitting them to appear only by the *borhsealdor* and four men of the *borgh*, except in the towns that answered by twelve men.[1]

Such regular attendance of the tithing favored corporate action in the performing of court duty. Thus, a tithing some-times acted as pledge for the prosecution of a case,[2] and paid the fine in the usual way when the cause turned out to be a bad one or when the prosecution was not regularly conducted. In some cases, as we have seen, it bailed a man from prison like an ordinary mainpernor; in others it stood as pledge for the payment of an amercement imposed upon some person, or even as pledge in the event of wager of law by the ordeal of hot iron.[3] A tithing might also act as suit to bear witness to a ques-tion of fact. Such an instance occurred in Somerset in 1225, when a tithing, along with twelve jurors, testified that the bailiff of the hundred told the truth in asserting that a certain man accused of causing a death confessed his guilt when first taken.[4] In a forest plea four tithings sometimes acted as main-pernors of a vill in which a dead deer had been found, and which accordingly had to clear itself from the accusation of poaching.[5] The chattels of a fugitive from justice, the booty dropped by robbers in their flight, or the *deodand* found near the dead, — things usually given into the keeping of the town-ship or the sheriff or some other responsible person to be brought before the justices in eyre for confiscation, — were in the south of England turned over to a tithing involved in the case.[6] For

---

[1] *Statutes of the Realm*, i. 223.
[2] Maitland, *Pleas of the Crown for Gloucester*, Nos. 114, 116.
[3] Maitland, *Select Pleas of the Crown*, No. 24 (Lincolnshire, A. D. 1202).
[4] Healey, *Somersetshire Pleas*, 50.
[5] Turner, *Select Pleas of the Forest*, 71–72 (Essex, A. D. 1240–1241).
[6] Maitland, *Pleas of the Crown for Gloucester*, Nos. 89, 147, 419; Healey,

neglect in producing the contraband articles at the proper time the tithing was amerced, just as the sheriff was fined for a similar fault. If it fell to the tithingman and the men of the township under his supervision to appraise the value of such goods, — and this would often be their duty in case they had appropriated or had forgotten to bring the chattels, — they were liable to another amercement if the justices believed that they had not set a sufficiently high value on what had been committed to their keeping.[1] Likewise, if they told an untruth about anything before the justices they were subjected to further amercement.[2]

All these miscellaneous duties connected with the regular justice of the kingdom the tithing performed in the thirteenth century. At the same period the frankpledge group was also burdened with some special obligations in the manorial leet and the sheriff's tourn. In 1227 entire tithings, under-pledges as well as capital ones, were required to make tri-weekly suit at a hundred court held by the bishop of Salisbury;[3] and even at the beginning of the fourteenth century the capital pledge in some cases performed a similar function at hundred courts.[4] Often a manorial tithing, one of whose number did not appear at the view of frankpledge as required, was ordered to produce the delinquent at the next view.[5] Tithings likewise acted as

---

Somersetshire Pleas, 246. That in the south and west this was often a real frankpledge, not merely a territorial, tithing is indicated by the following entry: "Gilo del Maine occidit Petrum de la Mote dominum suum et fugit . . . tunica ipsius Gilonis commissa fuit Decenne villate de Kinemereford habenda coram justiciariis" (Maitland, *Pleas for Gloucester,* No. 147). Compare "in franco plegio villate de Wudecestria" (*ibid.* No. 224). According to Assize Roll, No. 60, m. 22*b* (A. D. 1272), a tithing in Buckinghamshire, probably a mere frank-pledge group, accounts for the chattels of two men who have been imprisoned.

[1] Healey, *Somersetshire Pleas,* 267.
[2] *Ibid.* 37.
[3] *Bracton's Note Book,* ii. 195.
[4] Salt Archaeol. Soc., *Collections,* v. pt. i. 87.
[5] Maitland, *Select Pleas in Manorial Courts,* 94.

manucaptors, till the next court was held, for freemen as well as for bondmen who were presented in manorial courts for various defaults and were not there.[1] Such service, presupposing a general attendance of the tithing, was required well down into the fourteenth century.[2] On Berkshire manors, it is said, the whole tithing attended the view of frankpledge in 1441, and even as late as 1480;[3] but this probably means only that it had to be represented by the tithingman and perhaps four others at most.

One reason for the requirement of such attendance was that the tithing frequently made presentments of infractions of manorial usage.[4] More than this, it was often required to bring a certain sum of money with it to the view of frankpledge. In the south of England in the fifteenth century this was called "cert money." Given in the latter part of the thirteenth century nominally as a freewill offering of the tithing, and presented by the tithingman for meeting the expense of holding the "law day,"[5] it later became a fixed payment, and often included a certain number of quarters of wheat in addition to the pence rendered as cert money proper.[6] In Essex in the fourteenth century there was a similar payment, consisting regularly of one penny from every man in tithing.[7] Such a payment was usually made under the name of tithingpenny even in the reign of Henry II, as is shown by quittance of the obligation in royal charters.[8] It was stated as a grievance against the abbot of

---

[1] Young, *Dulwich College*, ii. 274.

[2] Clark, in *Eng. Hist. Review*, xix. 719.

[3] Hone, *The Manor and Manorial Records*, 156, 157, 160.

[4] Maitland, *Select Pleas in Manorial Courts*, 169; Hone, *The Manor*, etc., 164 (A. D. 1293), 155 (A. D. 1441).

[5] Hone, *The Manor*, etc., 147, 148.

[6] *Ibid.* 155, 157, 158, 160.

[7] Clark, in *Eng. Hist. Review*, xix. 715–718, xx. 483.

[8] Dugdale, *Monasticon*, iv. 515. It occurs also in what purports to be a charter grant of Henry I made in 1133, though there is question as to the text of the document (see *ibid.* vi. 296).

St. Augustine's, Canterbury, that tenants who were freemen of the city had to pay *borhfaldrespeni* in his halimote held in one of the suburbs, and were not permitted to be in frankpledge in the city.[1] By a Leicestershire customary of the early fourteenth century tithingpenny is defined as tallage of the tithing according to custom.[2] Originally it was a payment to the crown levied on the tithings by the sheriff, perhaps to meet the expenses of holding the view of frankpledge; and there were somewhat similar exactions on the ward and the hundred.[3] As the view itself tended more and more to pass into the hands of manorial lords by direct grant or by prescription, the new owners gained for their lands exemption from making such a payment to the fiscal agent of the king, and retained the fee themselves. Hence, from the circumstance that it was collected by the lord from the tithing, and that those in tithing were chiefly villains, the Leicestershire writer believed it to be a form of tallage. In the geldable parts of the county, tithingpenny was still collected at the end of the thirteenth century. In 1293, and at least for sixteen years previously, a Staffordshire villain who owed suit of sheriff's tourn paid two shillings for each of the semiannual sessions;[4] and on a Wiltshire manor at about the same time the payment was the same in amount.[5] Where the lord owed the usual mark annually for his view of frankpledge, the customary tenants are

[1] *Rot. Hundred.*, i. 203.

[2] Clark, in *Archaeologia*, xlvii. pt. i. 127. The editor's definition (*ibid.* 129) that it was a tax levied on the tithing by the sheriff seems hardly comprehensive enough for a period when the payment had in many cases passed into the hands of the lord of the manor.

[3] As in *Cockersand Chartulary* (Chetham Soc.), i. pt. i. 41.

[4] Salt Archaeol. Soc., *Collections*, vi. pt. i. 276.

[5] *Inquisitiones post Mortem for Wiltshire* (Wiltshire Archaeol. and Nat. Hist. Soc.), pt. iv. 228. It is interesting to observe that as early as 1219 this same amount was in some places collected for all in frankpledge who did not attend the view. See, for example, *Ramsey Chartulary* (Rolls Series), i. 491.

also found paying approximately half of the sum at each session.[1]

The tithing, whatever its size and whatever the principle upon which it was formed and named, was under the direction of a capital pledge (*plegius capitalis*), called also the tithingman (*decennarius*) or frankpledge, and in the days of the decline of the system the headbourow. In Kent, where a tithing was termed a *borg* (*borgha*), its head was known as the *borhsealdor* or *borgesheavod*. In a borough ward the alderman, besides fulfilling his ordinary duties, sometimes acted as head of the whole ward with reference to frankpledge business as well. During the thirteenth and fourteenth centuries tithings in Essex seem regularly to have had two capital pledges,[2] an arrangement occasioned perhaps by the needs of procedure in the local court. In the fourteenth century there were tithings without such officials at all;[3] but by that time the original character of frankpledge was somewhat changed.

Modern authorities are correct in agreeing that the capital pledge gained his place by election at the view of frankpledge.[4] Near the end of the thirteenth century the hundred of Calehill in Kent complained that a certain John Baldesert had designated John de Eversle to be *borgefaldr* (*borhsealdor*) without election of his *borh*.[5] On the manor of Wednesbury in Staf-

---

[1] *Cart. St. Peter of Gloucester* (Rolls Series), iii. 72. Cf. Willis-Bund, *Inquisitiones post Mortem for Worcester* (Worcestersh. Hist. Soc.), pt. i. 57.

[2] Turner, *Select Pleas of the Forest*, 71; Young, *Dulwich College*, ii. 285; Clark, in *Eng. Hist. Review*, xix. 715–719.

[3] Hudson, *Leet Jurisdiction in Norwich*, p. lvii. This seems to have been due to a general unwillingness to hold so burdensome an office. If there were not enough tithingmen at a Norwich leet to make presentments, men from the tithings were, as Hudson tells us, sworn to serve as capital pledges for the occasion.

[4] Stubbs, *Constitutional History*, i. 98; Vinogradoff, *Villainage*, 363.

[5] *Rot. Hundred.*, i. 212.

fordshire, which was of the ancient domain and had been in the hands of Henry II, it was lawful, according to a record of 1330, "for the lord of the manor to appoint provosts from year to year and tithingmen by election of their peers." [1] Before entering upon his duties the new capital pledge took oath that he would faithfully perform them. Election was for a one-year term; but it was customary to keep capital pledges in office several years in succession,[2] even though the position was one involving responsibilities which men were loath to assume. In the time of Edward I there was complaint in some quarters that bailiffs took money from certain men to remove them from the post and to put others in their places.[3] There was apparently an effort to have the most substantial men of the tithing in this office, and in boroughs like Norwich it was possible to secure persons of standing in the community.[4] The older men seem often to have served as heads of tithings, for not infrequently capital pledges are mentioned as having sons in their tithings. Yet, despite all precautions, it seems sometimes to have been impossible, especially in rural districts, where the tithings consisted largely or entirely of villains, to place worthy men at the

---

[1] Salt Archaeol. Soc., *Collections*, ix. 17. In the sixteenth century, election of the petty constable, the successor of the tithingman, was by presentment to the office in the court leet. See Cox, *Derbyshire*, 109.

[2] Reference, in the fifteenth century, to removal from office when an election takes place (Young, *Dulwich College*, ii. 281) even leads one to suspect that the chief pledge had to serve until formally removed by the court. In some districts capital pledges served nine or ten years (Maitland, *Court Baron*, 110). A fifteenth-century article of the leet, inquiring whether "any *hedborgh* of any other *lete* have become resident within this *lete*" (L. T. Smith, *Common-place Book*, 161), seems to warrant the inference that not even by removal from the manor might this official hope to be free from the duties of his post. According to Sir Thomas Smith, who died in 1577, petty constables were chosen by the homage, and kept their office three or four years, more or less, as the parish agreed (see his *Common-welth of England*, 98 [90]).

[3] *Rot. Hundred.*, i. 489.

[4] Hudson, *Leet Jurisdiction in Norwich*, p. lvii.

head of the tithings;[1] for more than once in the records the capital pledge appears as a criminal and a fugitive.

In the south and west of England the head of the frankpledge tithing was often village reeve as well; but this circumstance seems not to have affected his duties as capital pledge, though it is often difficult to determine in which capacity he is acting. The usual offices of the capital pledge were of two kinds, — those pertaining to the actual leadership of the tithing, and those connected with the presentment of offences and other matters at the view of frankpledge. The *Leges Edwardi* represent the head of the tithing as possessed of a judicial competence;[2] but this is only a legal fable.

In the first of the capacities mentioned the head man of the tithing seems clearly to have been the successor of the Anglo-Saxon tithingman, with whom he was identified by writers of the twelfth century.[3] As the tithingman in the time of Edgar led his men in the pursuit of a thief, so the tithingman of frankpledge days led those under his direction in apprehending known or suspected miscreants.[4] By the first quarter of the thirteenth century, though he still worked with the assistance of the men of his tithing, his position began more and more to resemble that of the constable of later days. The capital pledge was now subject to direction by the justices or by other officials, in that he had to receive into the custody of his tithing at their order accused persons who could not be put in prison in the regular way, or persons released from prison on bail,[5] or the chattels of fugi-

---

[1] In 1293 it is recorded that one Berkshire tithingman was a half-virgater, and that another was the tenant of a farthing land. See Maitland, *Select Pleas in Manorial Courts*, 165, 169.

[2] Ch. xxix, in Liebermann, *Gesetze*, i. 652.

[3] Thus in the pipe rolls of Henry II the-tithing is often called by the Latinized English name *tedinga*.

[4] Maitland, *Pleas of the Crown for Gloucester*, Nos. 262, 280, 410, 444.

[5] *Ibid.* Nos. 219, 227, 269.

tives.[1] Direction by a superior peace officer is also obvious in
cases in which the head of a tithing leads his men to attach the
person of a man clearly not in frankpledge who is formally
appealed for crime.[2] In addition to this subjection to the
justices, there was a similar responsibility to the coroner and the
sheriff. The fact that a tithing was present when the royal
bailiff of the hundred captured a man accused of homicide indicates clearly that the capital pledge, when in active pursuit of a
criminal, was subject to the orders of a superior local peace officer when one was present,[3] just as in the time of Edgar the
tithingman was summoned by the hundredman.

From the latter part of the thirteenth century capital pledges
served as petty constables without the aid of their tithings,[4] by
acting for them in arresting criminals and harborers of criminals,[5] by carrying out the orders of the sheriff in his tourn for
the remedying of purprestures and nuisances,[6] and by leading
criminals to prison either with or without his direct order.[7] In
the reign of Edward I they are to be found acting as *custodes
pacis*.[8] Before the middle of the next century, with the development of the system of justices of the peace and the regular appointment of two constables for each hundred according to a
provision of the Statute of Westminster in 1285, the heads of
tithings began to act regularly as assistant peace officers.[9] Thus

[1] Maitland, *Pleas of the Crown for Gloucester*, No. 147; Healey, *Somersetshire Pleas*, 246.

[2] Maitland, *Pleas of the Crown for Gloucester*, No. 101.

[3] Healey, *Somersetshire Pleas*, 50.

[4] Salt Archaeol. Soc., *Collections*, x. 5; Gross, *Select Coroners' Rolls*, 67.

[5] Maitland, *Court Baron*, 99.   [6] Fleta, 114.

[7] *Rot. Hundred.*, ii. 214; *Calendar of Patent Rolls*, Edw. II, 1313–1317,
pp. 504–505.

[8] According to Coram Rege Roll, No. 148 (24 Edw. I, Public Record Office),
two frankpledges of a vill in Nottingham acting in such a capacity seized into
the hands of the king the tenement of a man who had been executed.

[9] Gross, *Select Coroners' Rolls*, 67, 79.

the petty constables of Queen Elizabeth's time, "made and sworne at the leets of the lords,"[1] were often but the survivors of the capital pledges of the twelfth and thirteenth centuries.

The second category of duties pertaining to the head of the tithing — those connected more immediately with the view of frankpledge or court leet — are in general of considerably later origin than the offices just noted. Maitland has shown that the development of the procedure in these local courts was subsequent to the issue of the Assize of Clarendon, which established the sheriff's tourn in its later form and at the same time required that crimes be presented by twelve law-worthy men of the hundred and four of the vill.[2] The practice of the sheriff's tourn was imitated by lords of manors in their courts; and in course of time the capital pledges, who naturally knew about crimes in their own vills, were utilized to make the presentments taken on the occasion of the view of frankpledge, whether it was held in the sheriff's tourn or in the manorial leet, where the lord had the privilege of making the view. Such procedure did not, however, always excuse the whole tithing from attendance. When this was not required the capital pledge was often responsible for producing his men on a court day;[3] and in the fourteenth century they were even sworn to be justiciable by him.[4] Appearance on these two occasions each year to make presentments either at the tourn or at the leet thus came to be recognized as a characteristic feature of the capital pledge's duties before the reign of Edward I,[5] and seems to have been regarded as dating from that of Henry II.[6]

---

[1] Sir Thomas Smith, *Common-welth of England*, 98 (90). See also Lambard, *Constables*, 9.

[2] Maitland, *Select Pleas in Manorial Courts*, p. xxxi; Assize of Clarendon, chs. i, ix, x, in Stubbs, *Select Charters*, 143–144.

[3] Maitland, *Court Baron*, 140; Clark, in *Eng. Hist. Review*, xix. 719.

[4] Maitland, *Court Baron*, 101.

[5] *Plac. de Quo War.*, 1, 3, 12, 35, 183, 246, 295, 612, 774.

[6] *Ibid.* 506, 553.

After the time of Edward I the right to have presentments made by capital pledges was a prerogative of the king and of those who held view of frankpledge by his authority. In 1330 there was an instance in which a bailiff of the king, to settle a dispute, conceded that for a payment of twelve pence a year the heads of tithings of the manor of Clifton might make presentments every three weeks for hue and bloodshed in the court of the honor of Peverell at Nottingham.[1] The presentment of minor police matters by the capital pledges was an important, but not an essential, part of the procedure of the medieval court leet.

Although the responsibilities connected with the headship of a tithing were heavy, yet, so far as can be determined, the position brought no exemption from the financial liabilities of the ordinary member of a tithing. Whatever the nature of the default, the capital pledge was apparently amerced along with his associates. It may be said, however, on the other hand that, if through any negligence of his the tithing failed to perform its duty, all were still amerced in common. If the tithing incurred a pecuniary penalty, its head man was before the law but one member of the association; but his capability or incapability meant so much to the associates whom he directed that their influence must have been exerted to keep the best possible men in the position. In the fourteenth century, at least, a judicious capital pledge might by a small payment sometimes have a troublesome person transferred to another tithing,[2] the common burden of responsibility for producing him in case he turned criminal being thus lightened accordingly.

This head man, whose character was of such importance to his associates, also had responsibilities of his own which they

---

[1] *Plac. de Quo War.*, 612.
[2] Maitland, *Court Baron*, 140.

did not share. The direction of the numerous activities of the tithing was of itself likely to claim much of his time. Furthermore, his fourteenth-century function of paying in court regular sums of money due from the tithing,[1] when taken together with the fact that tithings were above all else expected to be obedient to their heads in the matter of financial contributions,[2] shows clearly enough that the collection from his associates of their part of the amercement levied upon the tithing was another duty with which he was charged. As late as 1439 the head of a Wiltshire tithing which failed to appear at the tourn and to pay the cert silver was to be punished by confinement in the castle of Sarum till he rendered satisfaction.[3] For not attending the view of frankpledge to make presentments there was of course a fine; and for failure to present offences (concealment), or for bringing false presentment, there were other amercements awaiting the jury of capital pledges.[4] At the end of the thirteenth century the peasant head of a tithing who in the discharge of his duty took a criminal to a castle for incarceration was in some districts fortunate if he was not compelled by an overbearing official to make him a money payment for receiving the prisoner. Under such circumstances, the imprisonment of a capital pledge for a few days to make him submissive was not an unknown measure.[5]

[1] Kitchin, *Manor of Manydown* (Hampshire Record Soc.), 134–135 (A. D. 1365); Young, *Dulwich College*, ii. 274. In *Rot. Hundred.*, i. 98, is a complaint that in Dorset a man takes money for a felony from men not of his "*decena de Porstoke*" (Poorstock, or Powerstock).

[2] See above, p. 90.

[3] *Wiltshire Archaeol. and Nat. Hist. Magazine*, xiii. 114.

[4] Hudson, *Leet Jurisdiction in Norwich*, 11, 12, 14, 22, 44. For concealment in the Bishop of Ely's court at Littleport in 1325 twelve free jurors were amerced two shillings, and twelve capital pledges twelve pence (Maitland, *Court Baron*, 140).

[5] *Rot. Hundred.*, i. 91, 181; ii. 214.

So unpopular did the combination of these features render the office of chief pledge that men would gladly have escaped it; but one had to serve when chosen. In the reign of Edward II the bishop of Oxford counted among his liberties the right to have *decenarii* for the hamlet of Westington in Suffolk by election of the tenants. Any one elected *ex officio terrae suae pertinente* had to serve, on penalty of paying two shillings.[1] Sometimes the person chosen tried to shirk the responsibility by refusing to be sworn; but for this evasion there was also an amercement which often resulted in a man's changing his mind and taking the oath.[2] In the leet of the fifteenth century a capital pledge sometimes secured removal from his office by a payment of from six to eighteen pence;[3] and it may be assumed that, for the period before the end of the thirteenth century, when a villain was expected to hold a manorial office to which he was elected unless he rendered satisfaction to the lord, the capital pledge could be excused from serving on no easier condition. A suggestion of one possible pretext for not fulfilling the duties of the position after induction into office comes from Gloucestershire about 1220, when a certain Philip "*la prophete*," to the custody of whose tithing an accused member had been committed, declared that he could not produce the man before the justices because he had assumed the cross. After he had set out, however, ostensibly on his crusade, the jurors suspected that this was but a ruse, and the justices in eyre required the tithing to produce Philip as well as the man committed to its custody.[4] If one

---

[1] Public Record Office, Coram Rege Roll, No. 225, m. 110.

[2] Hudson, *Leet Jurisdiction in Norwich*, 7, and cf. 18. Young (*Dulwich College*, ii. 285) gives a case in a court roll of the year 1410. As late as 1660 a man was fined for refusing to serve as headborough for Dulwich Manor (*ibid.* 271).

[3] *Ibid.* 282; Clark, in *Eng. Hist. Review*, xix. 718.

[4] Maitland, *Pleas of the Crown for Gloucester*, No. 241.

may form a conclusion from this solitary instance, one may affirm that the capital pledge who fled to escape his duties to the royal courts was dealt with exactly like a fugitive criminal.

A review of the history of the tithing shows, then, that the arrangement was instituted as a means of preserving the national peace. Maintained at first exclusively by the activity of a royal official, the tithing performed its duties in connection with the system of local courts and the sessions of the king's itinerant justices, and in some cases even in conjunction with the central courts at Westminster. By the thirteenth century, however, it was in many cases sustained by a manorial court, in which it came to discharge a large part of its ordinary duty; and in the succeeding century the same process went on to a greater and greater extent. In the fifteenth century, although the head man retained his functions connected with the maintenance of the national peace, the tithing itself, as the sheriff's tourn declined, came to be mentioned only in the court that had competence pertaining to the manor. In order to understand how this process of decline was brought about it is necessary to study, first, the development of the manorial leet from the view of frank-pledge, and, secondly, the new system of enforcing peace observance which sprang up after the late thirteenth century, topics that will be discussed in the next two chapters.

CHAPTER IV

VIEW OF FRANKPLEDGE

AFTER considering who the members of the tithing were and what its functions and obligations, one must inquire into the legal processes and constitutional arrangements through which its perpetuity was secured and at the same time much of its activity discharged. A system of suretyship which was depended upon to keep in order the masses of the English people was an institution that demanded regular national provision for its maintenance and supervision. This provision, as long as it existed, bore standing testimony to the importance of the system, and its decline was good evidence that reliance was no longer put on that method of securing an observance of the peace.

As early as the reign of Edgar, and almost certainly still earlier in the time of Athelstan, the maintenance of *borh* for peace observance was intrusted to the court of the hundred.[1] When Canute re-enacted a law to enforce such suretyship upon freemen generally, he was careful to provide that they must all be brought into some hundred.[2] There is no direct means of determining whether matters affecting the maintenance of the general *borh* system were taken up at any meeting of the hundred court, or whether they were dealt with at certain sessions only. The fact, however, that mainpast suretyship was pro-

---

[1] See above, p. 26, note 1.
[2] See above, p. 28, note 1.

vided by Anglo-Saxon law for temporary sojourners must have limited the necessity of considering such business to a very few sessions each year, held at intervals just close enough together to prevent the youth who arrived at the age of legal accountability from escaping too long from his new obligation to be in *borh* and to make oath promising neither to be a thief nor to be cognizant of theft.[1] In the reign of Henry I, after *borh* had been reorganized into frankpledge, it was the practice to hold two special sessions of the hundred each year for the transaction of this and other kinds of business; and a century later in Magna Carta there is clear intimation that at least since 1166 these special sessions had been held, one in the spring and one in the autumn.[2] Such arrangements seem so clearly in accord with the needs of the *borh* system in the reign of Canute that one can hardly doubt their existence, at least as early as his efforts to reorganize that system after the disorder of Ethelred's reign.[3]

The special sessions of the hundred for putting men in frankpledge were ordained by decree of Henry II to be held by the sheriffs throughout the realm, except, as it appears, in the case of towns and boroughs, which were required to maintain for their men either frankpledge or a kindred form of suretyship.[4] The innovation here, one is to understand, was not the sheriff's connection with the business, but the sweeping extension of his competence in the matter to private lands and jurisdictions, — perhaps the same sort of change which Canute wished to make when he required that all men should not only be in *borh* but

---

[1] 2 Canute, xxi, in Liebermann, *Gesetze*, i. 324-325.

[2] Magna Carta of 1217, ch. xlii, *Statutes of the Realm*, i. 17-19. Cf. Assize of Clarendon, chs. ix, x, in Stubbs, *Select Charters*, 144.

[3] Since writing the above, the writer has observed with interest that Professor Hearnshaw (*Leet Jurisdiction in England*, 68) is also impressed with the probability of the existence of such a "view" in Anglo-Saxon times.

[4] Assize of Clarendon, chs. ix, x, in Stubbs, *Select Charters*, 144.

should also be brought into the hundred courts. That the sheriff presided over such sessions of the hundred from a period but shortly after the Conqueror's day, there can hardly be a doubt.[1] Not only was he the logical person to give supervision to the courts held in the hundred, but he was the fiscal agent of the crown for the county, which is but another way of expressing the same idea; for the object in maintaining jurisdiction in Norman England was not power so much as revenue. The hundred court, which was the principal criminal tribunal of the land, was one of the most promising sources of income, a fact which, in the reign of William Rufus and in the early part of that of Henry I, had led the sheriff to summon it, as well as the county court, at other times and in other places than had been customary before the Conquest. The latter king, in ordering that these irregularities should not occur except in cases of the king's financial necessity, was careful to add in words which again remind one of Canute's enactment, that all in the county should come to the county and hundred courts as in the time of Edward the Confessor, so that none might disturb the king's peace and order through failure to follow his pleas and observe his judgments.[2] If the king would thus compel his vassals and their vassals to adjudicate their cases in his courts for the benefit of his exchequer, as was clearly his aim in this decree, it may safely be assumed that he would be inclined to have his sheriffs attend the hundred courts for the purpose of preserving the

---

[1] Hearnshaw, after taking the position that the view of frankpledge was held by the hundredor, is later convinced that it was the sheriff who in the Norman period took the view through the hundreds (see his *Leet Jurisdiction*, 66, 337, and note). The well-known writ of Henry I shows conclusively that it was the sheriff who at that time convened the hundred for the purposes of royal business. See next note; also above, p. 60, note 1.

[2] Writ of Henry (between 1109 and 1111) to Bishop Sampson and Sheriff Urso d'Abitot of Worcester, in Stubbs, *Select Charters*, 103–104; also in Liebermann, *Gesetze*, i. 524. See Adams, in *Amer. Hist. Review*, viii. 487.

sources of considerable revenue arising from the suretyship responsibility of the peasants.

There were numerous occasions upon which the Norman sheriff might collect sums of money at the view of frankpledge, for to maintain the frankpledge system amercements were of course necessary. The tithing or the tithingman who failed in any way to discharge the responsibilities of the office was punished by a fine, which in the early twelfth century, as well as in Saxon days, was a heavy one when a man under suretyship fled for crime. Another available source of profit to a king who demanded for himself alone the right of punishing breach of *borh* on the ground that it concerned the general peace and security which he had promised,[1] lay in the failure of a vill to have its residents in tithing, a duty that was plainly hinted at in the time of Henry I, just as it was clearly stated at a later day.[2] One may, therefore, accept without qualification Maitland's assertion that at least as early as the time of Henry I the sheriff presided over two sessions of the hundred a year (when as many were deemed necessary), which all freemen were to attend in order that inquiry might be made whether the tithings were full, or who for any reason had been dropped from any of them or had been out of tithing since the last view.[3]

Inference may also be drawn for a still earlier time. In the fact that information as to view of frankpledge comes subsequently to the coronation charter of Henry I ordering the courts to be held as prior to the Conquest, and that persistent tradition,

---

[1] *Leges Henrici*, viii. 1, in Liebermann, *Gesetze*, i. 554; and see Charter of Liberties, ch. xii, in Stubbs, *Select Charters*, 101.

[2] *Leges Edw. Conf.*, xx. 1, in Liebermann, *Gesetze*, i. 645.

[3] Maitland, *Select Pleas in Manorial Courts*, p. xxxiii; *Leges Henrici*, viii. 2, in Liebermann, *Gesetze*, i. 554.

current within a generation of the Conqueror's death,[1] ascribes to William himself the same sort of decree, with the additional requirement that every man have sureties to lead him to justice, there seems to be evidence confirmatory of the surmise that such sessions had been the normal order, at least from the time of Canute.[2] It may further be assumed that they had been held by the sheriff ever since the reorganization of his office in its fiscal appointments soon after the Conquest. Before that time they were probably called by a royal reeve of the hundred, who had, among other duties, that of putting men under suretyship, and who appears in Domesday as well as in the laws of Edgar, Ethelred, and Canute.[3]

This semiannual tour of inspection, the regularity of which had been interrupted by the anarchy of Stephen's reign, but which Henry II had restored and by the decree of 1166 reorganized, — at the same time, in accordance with his custom, pushing its authority as far as possible beyond its former limits, — had by the early thirteenth century received the name by which it is known in law, that of the sheriff's tourn.

Such an extraordinary session of the hundred, one object of which was peace maintenance through suretyship, very easily came to deal also with pleas involving infractions of the peace, as well as with those concerning local trespasses and disputes. Although the writer of the *Leges Edwardi* is not always good

---

[1] *Willelmi I Articuli X* (1110–1135), viii, viii. 1, in Liebermann, *Gesetze,* i. 488; French *Articuli* of William (1192–1193), *ibid.* 489; *Leis Willelme* (1090–1135, probably 1100–1120), xx. 3*a*, *ibid.* 506.

[2] The assumption of older writers (see Powell, *Antiquity of the Leet,* 13) that the tourn of the sheriff and the view of frankpledge were instituted by Alfred, rests upon the fabulous statements of the *Mirror of Justices.* See above, pp. 6–7.

[3] Stubbs, *Constitutional History,* i. 113, and notes; Liebermann, *Ueber die Leges Edw. Conf.,* 64. Thus the convener of the hundred court in Saxon England could hardly have been the popular hundredman, or hundredealdor. He was evidently a royal official.

authority, he nevertheless shows familiarity with an undoubted jurisdiction of the hundred court when he represents the hundred as making *forisfacturas, emendationes,* and *ordinationes* in cases between neighbors concerning pastures, meadows, and boundaries, as well as in many other such matters.[1] This duality of purpose is brought out by the second Magna Carta of Henry III, which directs the tourn to be held "that our peace may be observed and that the tithing may be intact as it was wont to be."[2] Greater as well as lesser crimes had of old been punished in the hundred. In the reign of Henry I the view of frankpledge at the half-yearly sessions was only one of the items of business; but when Henry II introduced into the sheriff's semiannual visitation of the hundreds the presentment jury and communal accusation of offences in place of private appeal, which was as perilous to the accuser as to the accused, the result was a greatly increased number of pleas at such sessions. After 1166 a jury composed of twelve men of the hundred and four of the township was sworn before the sheriff to present those in their community who were suspected of being robbers, murderers, thieves, or receivers of such criminals, that they might be reported at the sessions of the justices.[3] Such a mode of presentment came to be followed for lesser offences also, those accused of such faults being tried and amerced by the sheriff, who seems to be the only judge mentioned.[4]

This jurisdiction rapidly gained in importance until it overshadowed that of the older semiannual session. Maitland is

---

[1] *Leges Edw. Conf.,* xxviii, xxix, in Liebermann, *Gesetze,* i. 651–652. It is probable that even in the reign of Henry I the capital pledges served as constables to carry out the court's orders.

[2] Magna Carta of 1217, ch. xlii, *Statutes of the Realm,* i. 17–19; Stubbs, *Select Charters,* 346.

[3] Assize of Clarendon, ch. i, in Stubbs, *Select Charters,* 143.

[4] Pollock and Maitland, *English Law* (1895), i. 547.

thus substantially correct when he contends that the sheriff's tourn begins with the Assize of Clarendon in 1166;[1] for, although the sheriff had long before that time made his round of the hundreds, his earlier jurisdiction had neither the character nor the importance of the institution known in legal history by the name of tourn. View of frankpledge is not found in charters prior to this date, for the reason that as a franchise it did not yet exist. The norm for its legal exercise, when it first appears in the early thirteenth century, is always the mode employed in the reign of Henry II. So considerable a source of revenue was to be derived from this jurisdiction that there was constant temptation for the sheriff to make his tourn oftener than twice a year. Among the concessions that it was deemed necessary to make in the king's name in 1217 in order to guarantee the rights of the baronial party and to win back its allegiance to the crown, was a clause in the Magna Carta of that year limiting the number of tourns which the sheriff might make to the two a year which had been customary for at least a century. At only one of these sessions, however, that after Michaelmas — the other was held after Easter — was the view of frankpledge thenceforth to have a place.[2]

Since the view, which had formerly been part of the business at both sessions, was now to be made at only one, some confusion of terms naturally resulted, the old name of view of frankpledge being often applied to the tourn in general. The very justices of the bench were no more explicit in 1231 than to say that, by the Great Charter, sheriffs took view of frankpledge and attachments twice a year;[3] and even when pains

---

[1] *Select Pleas in Manorial Courts*, pp. xxxiii–xxxvi.

[2] Magna Carta of 1217, ch. xlii, *Statutes of the Realm*, i. 17–19; Stubbs, *Select Charters*, 346.

[3] *Bracton's Note Book*, ii. 402. Maitland (*Select Pleas in Manorial Courts*, p. xxix) has pointed out that even in Coke's day the official style of the tourn

were taken to use the term in a more exact sense the distinction was not an easy one to make. Britton says that the particular session of the court which before the sheriff was called the tourn, where a special inquiry was made concerning those not in tithing, was even in royal hundreds commonly called view of frankpledge.[1] In East England it was called the leet.[2] None of the writers of the thirteenth century except Britton considered it worth while to give the procedure of the view of frankpledge proper as distinct from that of the rest of the tourn. Those who were required to be present at both kinds of sessions were the same persons; and the inquiry concerning those not in tithing was made by presentment, just as was that relating to the other matters taken up at the court. View of frankpledge, then, in the ordinary sense of the term, meant not only the actual inquiry as to who was, and who was not, in tithing, but also the entire jurisdiction of the sheriff in the tourn.

The mandate of the Magna Carta of 1217 was by no means sufficient to prevent the sheriff from holding more sessions of the hundred in his county than those therein provided, or from holding them at different times. That the subject was a live one for more than three-quarters of a century is witnessed by the incorporation of the same safeguards in reissues of the charter up to 1297. It was a matter of law, repeated in royal writ and in statute, which still needed emphasis at the end of the thirteenth century, that the king had " his court in tourns and views of hundreds twice a year and not oftener as by the Great Charter."[3] At the very end of the century it was still

was "curia visus franci plegii domini regis apud B coram vicecomite in turno suo" (Coke, *Fourth Institute*, 260-265).

[1] Britton, i. 178, and see also 181.

[2] Rye, *North Erpingham*, pt. i. 219; *Rot. Hundred.*, i. 442, 470.

[3] Letter of Henry III to sheriffs respecting hundreds and wapentakes, A. D. 1234, *Annales Monastici* (Rolls Series), iii. 140; Statute of Marlborough, A. D. 1267, *Statutes of the Realm*, i. 22.

seasonable for the compiler of laws to repeat, in the words of that revered document, that "No bailiff or sheriff ought to hold tourn in the hundred except twice a year, only in due and accustomed place once after Easter, and again after the feast of St. Michael. View of frankpledge is to be without exaction, so that each may have the liberties which he has by just title or was wont to have in the time of Henry II or later has rightly acquired." [1]   In the time of Edward I the itinerant justices seem to have been charged with the duty of making special inquiry as to who had made his tourn more than twice a year and at what time.[2]   In 1357 there were still grievances in regard to the same points, the Commons complaining that the sheriffs made their tourns oftener than permitted by the Great Charter, and that they went "oftentimes in Lent, when men ought to intend devotion and other works of charity for remedy of their souls, and sometimes after the Gule of August, when every man almost is occupied about the cutting and entring of his corn." The result was a statute declaring that the sheriff who made his tourn except within the month after Easter and the month after Michaelmas should lose the tourn for that time.[3]

What aggravated this irregularity and oppression connected with the tourn and view of frankpledge was the system of farming both the counties and the hundreds. As the sheriff was obviously unable to attend two sessions of every hundred in his county, especially after the great rush of business which followed the changes of 1166, he frequently turned the hundred over to a bailiff, exacting from him a farm that would yield a good profit over and above the farm which he himself paid to the exchequer for his county. The bailiff was therefore inclined

---

[1] Fleta, 112.

[2] Articles of eyre under King Edward, *Statutes of the Realm*, i. 235.

[3] *Ibid.* 352.

to hold court as often as possible and to collect as heavy fines and dues as he could in order to reimburse himself; moreover, he was far more likely to be a man who knew how to make financial exactions than to be one who knew law. The Great Charter of 1215 aimed to correct these evils by providing that hundreds should be let at the ancient ferm without increment, and that the royal sheriffs and bailiffs should be persons who knew the law of the realm and meant rightly to observe it.[1] A full century later, in the reign of Edward II, a second attempt was made to remedy the abuses by the passing, in 1316, of the Second Statute of Sheriffs, which, though it really accomplished little, revealed the evils of the system. It provided that hundred courts, whether they belonged to the king or not, were to be held by able persons of standing who had land in the hundred, or in the shire in which the hundred was located; that sheriffs or hundredors who were insufficient were to be removed; that hundredors to whom the execution of writs directed to the sheriff was intrusted were to be known and sworn in full county; and that hundreds were to be leased and bailed to such persons for a reasonable rent so that they need not use extortion because of "too outrageous a ferm." [2] All these provisions had to be re-enacted under Edward III in 1329, and part of them again in 1337.[3] Under their operation the person who held the view of frankpledge was likely to be a knight of the shire,[4] belonging to the same social class as the justices of the peace. It was not till 1403 that the sheriff was forbidden by law to farm his balliwick,[5] and not till 1445 that he was prohibited from

---

[1] Chs. xxv, xlv, *Statutes of the Realm*, i. 6–7; Stubbs, *Select Charters*, 300, 302.
[2] *Statutes of the Realm*, i. 175.
[3] *Ibid.* 258 (Statute of Northampton), 277.
[4] See Salt Archaeol. Soc., *Collections*, xiii. 60.
[5] 4 Hen. IV, ch. v, *Statutes of the Realm*, ii. 134.

letting out to farm in any way either his county or any of his balliwicks, hundreds, or wapentakes.[1]

According to the writers of the thirteenth century, the suitors at the tourn were all the men of the hundred. Even in the early twelfth century the attendance at the semiannual views of frankpledge was greater than that at the ordinary hundred; all freemen, hearthfast as well as followers, were expected to be present.[2] The form of summons issued in the early part of the thirteenth century was directed to "all free tenants and others of the hundred."[3] Britton says that, being summoned, all freemen of the hundred and other landholders, except clerks, persons in religion, and women, were in general bound to appear; and he later shows that the tithings had duties, and consequently were expected to be present.[4] The *Mirror of Justices*, usually a very poor authority on constitutional history, is on some points in regard to this matter more accurate than Britton. The writer of this treatise knew that to the earlier rule, which required all free tenants to come to the tourn by service of their fees, exceptions had been made by Henry III;[5] and he was familiar with that part of the Statute of Marlborough,[6] taken over from the Provisions of 1259,[7] which excused from attendance archbishops, bishops, abbots, priors, earls, barons, men of religion, and women, unless their presence was especially required. With these exceptions, those whose attendance at the annual view of frankpledge he regarded as obligatory were not only the free tenants, but all men of the hundred, strangers as well as denizens, of the age of twelve years and above, except knights, deaf mutes, sick folk, idiots, lepers, and those in tithing

---

[1] 23 Hen. VI, ch. ix, *Statutes of the Realm*, ii. 334–337.
[2] *Leges Henrici*, viii, in Liebermann, *Gesetze*, i. 554.
[3] See Appendix A, below.   [4] Britton, i. 178.
[5] *Mirror*, 38.   [6] *Statutes of the Realm*, i. 22.
[7] *Ibid.* 9.

elsewhere.[1] For some reason he exempts only married women, a rule which may, like all that he says on this point, be merely local in its application. That all those in frankpledge were expected to attend the view seems to be a fair inference from the *Mirror*, as well as from Britton.[2] Maitland has called attention to the fact that in the apocryphal Statute of View of Frankpledge a tithing was considered to be sufficiently represented by its head.[3] According to Britton, inquiry was directed only to the question whether the headboroughs (*borhs*) had come to the view;[4] but according to Fleta it was also asked whether they had their tithings,[5] an inquiry the significance of which Maitland finds in the fact that a small payment of head money (*capitagium*, *chevagium*) was made by capital pledges that the men of their tithings might not be called by name.[6] The capital pledges of course had to attend in order to present offences. There is also evidence to show that at the tourn a vill was often represented by the conventional four men and the reeve.[7] Such was the form of representation for the tithing in the south of England, which corresponded in many cases to a township. In some instances either the capital pledge or the reeve and four men might do suit for a lord's holding.[8]

Summons to the tourn, in the early part of the reign of Henry III, directed all free tenants and others of the hundred to appear at the place and time set by the sheriff for the tendering to him of pleas and attachments pertaining to the crown, and for the presenting of view of frankpledge as in the time of

---

[1] *Mirror*, 39.   [2] Britton, i. 178.
[3] *Statutes of the Realm*, i. 246.   [4] Britton, i. 181.
[5] Fleta, 112.
[6] Maitland, *Select Pleas in Manorial Courts*, p. xxxi.
[7] *Rot. Hundred.*, i. 100, 101, 141, ii. 469; *Plac. de Quo War.*, 10, 254, 293.
[8] *Plac. de Quo War.*, 10.

Henry II.[1] If one may believe the *Mirror of Justices*, essoins were allowed for excusing the absence of those who could not come, and such essoins might be adjourned to the next ensuing court.[2] The same work also says that persons exempt from suits in inferior courts were not obliged to come themselves, unless their presence was necessary for some other purpose than for making the view.[3] As early as 1236 there was a statutory provision that every freeman who owed suit to the county, riding, hundred, wapentake, or court of his lord might "freely make his attorney do those suits for him";[4] and it is not improbable that several persons were represented by the same attorney, an arrangement that would have greatly reduced the number of persons ordinarily in attendance.

Accusations were made in the tourn in the form of presentments in answer to certain articles which the sheriff laid before jurors. Those requiring record were entered by the coroners of the county,[5] to be reported subsequently at the eyre. In 1285 the Second Statute of Westminster, following the usage of the reign of Henry II, provided that indictments in the tourn must be made on the oaths of at least twelve men.[6] The writers of the later thirteenth century also follow the practice of the preceding century in holding that such inquiries must be made by the oaths of twelve free men; for a serf could not indict a free man.[7] Pollock and Maitland explain the origin of presentment

---

[1] See Appendix A, below. In a charter concerning a private view it is provided that the view be held "at reasonable summons" of the bailiffs (*Cart. St. Peter of Gloucester*, Rolls Series, ii. 36).

[2] *Mirror*, 41.

[3] *Ibid.* 38.

[4] Statute of Merton, *Statutes of the Realm*, i. 4.

[5] See Appendix A, below.

[6] Ch. xiii, *Statutes of the Realm*, i. 81; Assize of Clarendon, ch. i, in Stubbs, *Select Charters*, 143.

[7] *Mirror*, 39; Assize of Northampton, ch. i, in Stubbs, *Select Charters*, 151.

through capital pledges by the suggestion that "under the influence of the Assize of Clarendon the duty of producing one's fellow-pledges to answer accusations seems to have been enlarged into duty of reporting their offences, of making presentments of all that went wrong in the tithing." [1] Before 1166 the capital pledges may, as Hearnshaw supposes, have answered questions concerning crimes in their tithings; but they could not, as he clearly shows, have had the power to make accusations against freemen.[2] In the later thirteenth century the capital pledges and the townships, after being sworn, usually gave their verdicts to a jury of twelve free men, who, having accepted those which they considered true and supplied any omissions that had been made,[3] handed over their presentments in final form to the sheriff. In the early part of the century a royal writ of summons seems to have been regarded as necessary before a freeman could be put on oath. In the time of Edward I, however, it was held that, inasmuch as this was "the king's day," instituted for the good of the public peace, persons might be sworn without the king's writ in the sheriff's tourns and at view of frankpledge as well as at the coroner's inquest and before the itinerant justices.[4] As a matter of fact, whatever jurists of this reign may say concerning the necessity of presentment in the tourn by twelve free jurors, there are records of quo warranto pleas before the royal justices in which presentments made by chief pledges alone appear as a matter of course.[5] No doubt there were instances in which twelve free jurors would not be present.

---

[1] Pollock and Maitland, *English Law* (1895), i. 557.
[2] Hearnshaw, *Leet Jurisdiction in England*, 68.
[3] Britton, i. 181; Fleta, 113. See, however, Hearnshaw, *Leet Jurisdiction*, 70.
[4] Fleta, 113; Britton, i. 9.
[5] *Plac. de Quo War.*, 88. Hearnshaw (*Leet Jurisdiction*, 67–71) seems to have the correct explanation when he contends that the presentments of the

Intimation of the exact process of holding view of frankpledge in the tourn comes chiefly from the articles upon which
the sheriff required the jurors to make inquest. Most of such
lists as have been preserved are to be found as part of, and
sometimes scattered among, the items of the larger list used at
the tourn in general. The very small number of matters concerning which the sheriff was to have inquiry made in 1166 had
in the course of a century and a quarter become enormously
increased. The sets that are extant, besides giving the articles
in a different order, give different articles, a circumstance
which seems to warrant the inference of Maitland not only that
these articles, like those of the eyre, were increased from time
to time by direction of the king and council, but that the sheriffs
were permitted to use any articles which they considered necessary for securing presentment of whatever was against the
king's peace.[1] The *Mirror of Justices* adds at the end of
its list, "and all other articles which may avail for the de-
struction of sin." [2] Yet it seems evident that in the reign
of Edward I certain lords, who professed to use the same
articles as those of the sheriff's tourn, had a very definite list
in mind.

In general it is possible to classify the business of the tourn,
outside of view of frankpledge proper, under the same two
heads as in the time of Henry II. There were, first, pleas of the
crown, presentments of which were to be reported to the justices. Among many such pleas mentioned about 1290, those
concerning burglary, robbery, theft, counterfeiting, homicide,
arson, and the abetting and receiving of persons guilty of such

capital pledges and those of the twelve free jurors represent two separate systems, the former dating from before 1166, the latter from that year, and the
latter tending to supersede the former.

[1] Maitland, *Select Pleas in Manorial Courts*, pp. xxxii-xxxiii.

[2] *Mirror*, 40.

offences,[1] show that, although the business of the tourn had
increased, its function of bringing accusations for the greater
sins against the king's peace was a very important one. A second category of articles had to do with minor police offences.
Besides the old-time inquiry concerning landmarks removed,
highways obstructed, waters diverted, and other such misdeeds
committed within a year and a day,[2] the more prominent articles,
usually common to the various lists, call for inquiry concerning
bloodshed, hue and cry wrongfully raised or not followed, pleas
of forbidden distress or other matters against bail and pledge,
and infractions of the assizes of bread and beer, cloths and
measures.[3]

The supervision of frankpledge within the hundred was, as
already observed, a special item of business at the Michaelmas
tourn, which from this circumstance was termed the view of
frankpledge to distinguish it from the session at Easter. When
the sheriff assembled the men of the hundred after Michaelmas,
besides laying before the jurors the two kinds of articles just
enumerated, he submitted to them a third set upon which they
were to hold inquest in order that presentment might be made
whether there had been any shirking of the obligation of frankpledge suretyship. As given by Britton, the list of these particular subjects of inquiry seems to be substantially that used at the
end of the thirteenth century. According to it the jurors presented upon oath (1) whether all the headboroughs had come

---

[1] Fleta, 112. Britton (i. 179) also includes inquiry concerning traitors,
sorcerers, apostates, heretics, and usurers.

[2] Fleta, 114.

[3] Britton, i. 181; Fleta, 112; *Mirror of Justices*, 39; *Statutes of the Realm*,
i. 57, 246 (Statute of Wales, and the so-called Statute concerning Frankpledge);
Maitland, *Court Baron*, 87; *Cart. St. Peter of Gloucester* (Rolls Series), iii. 221.
Cf. also "Capitula de Hokeday," in Dugdale, *Monasticon*, ii. 83. Hearnshaw
(*Leet Jurisdiction*, 43–64) gives a useful summary of various lists of articles
from the thirteenth to the fifteenth century.

to the view, and whether they had their tithings complete;
(2) the names of those who were twelve years old, and of their
receivers, or of those who had them in mainpast; (3) a report of vagrants of suspicious character who were not in mainpast.[1] In those cases in which the men of a tithing were still
expected to come to the view in a body there was also special
inquest to learn who had failed to appear; and near the end of
the thirteenth century, at least about London, the jurors seem
to have made presentment whether or not all in the hundred or
fee above the age of twelve had sworn fealty to the king, and
who had knowingly received those who had not done so.[2]

The real basis of this procedure was the information given by
the heads of tithings and the men of the township. In frankpledge presentments, as in other kinds, the twelve jurors, in
addition to their own knowledge, had the sworn testimony of
representatives of the tithings and vills who were present, and
who were strictly accountable for the correctness of the information which they gave. The capital pledge knew that his
answer upon oath to the inquiry whether all his men who
ought to be present were on hand could easily be verified by
reference to the tithing-list. The reeve and four from the township, or territorial tithing, knew that, should they fail to report
a man who was out of tithing, they would be held responsible,
and that, should such a person commit a crime indictable before the justices, the whole township would be amerced for
receiving him out of tithing. It was in the interest of the individual, as well as of his community, to see that the facts
were fully and correctly given.

Upon these presentments the business of the view proceeded.
Those who had not come as they ought, those who had failed
to have their tithings come as they ought, those above the age

---

[1] Britton, i. 181.   [2] *Mirror of Justices*, 39.

of twelve who had neglected to present themselves for enrolment in tithings, were all amerced.[1] Such persons as were
present and were not yet in frankpledge were duly enrolled.

Just how it was decided in what particular tithing a man
should be placed is a question that can be answered only by
conjecture. In the south and much of the west the matter was
determined by a person's residence. Elsewhere the careful
inquiry by jurors whether the tithings were full was obviously
designed to show what groups were in danger of becoming inef-
fective because of insufficient numbers. In such tithings either
youths or new-comers must be enrolled, or members of other
groups must be transferred to them. The fact, already noted,
that in some cases capital pledges secured changes in the per-
sonnel of their tithings by making small payments in manorial
courts, seems to show that the steward had power to place a
man in whatever tithing he chose;[2] and, if the manorial steward
had such power at a private view of frankpledge, the sheriff or
bailiff of the hundred must have had the same right. Tithing-
lists of the fourteenth century, however, show that it was not
then customary to even up tithings by taking men from the
larger and putting them into the smaller ones.[3] The location of
a laborer's house, and the place where he ordinarily worked
during the day, determined the degree of ease with which he
was able to join with others in a pursuit when the hue and cry
was raised. Since the same house and the same land were held
by successive generations of a peasant family, a given frank-

---

[1] Fleta, 114.

[2] A charter of the abbot of Cirencester, about 1225, provided that "whoever
wishes to enter or leave a tithing shall enter or leave before our bailiffs at the
two annual views of frankpledge" (*Cart. St. Peter of Gloucester*, Rolls Series,
ii. 35–36).

[3] See Clark, in *Eng. Hist. Review*, xix. 715–719. Tithings on an Essex
manor which in 1329 numbered respectively 13, 6, 5, 8, 9, 7, in 1337 numbered
1, 2, 7, 5, 6, 8, 8; and in 1343, 11, 8, 6, 7. See also above, p. 88.

9

pledge must usually have consisted of the men of a few families of near neighbors. In course of time a certain section of a village no doubt tended to constitute a tithing, just as a certain district in a town or a borough often did.[1]

The formality of putting a man in tithing began by administering to him the oath of fealty to the king and his heirs, and the old oath neither to be a thief nor to consent to theft,[2] — the former the precursor of what is termed by Powell "an oath for the demonstration of their natural legiance,"[3] the latter a requirement which had probably been observed continuously from the time of Canute.[4] After the oath the names of those entering frankpledge were enrolled upon the tithing-lists, a service for which it was customary, at least as early as 1198 and probably much earlier, to pay the clerk a penny for each person.[5] Some exhortation to refrain from crime and from the company of criminals seems to have followed this ceremony, together with an injunction to each man to obey his capital pledge.[6]

The relation of the view of frankpledge to mainpast is difficult to determine. It was necessary to know whether a man was in the latter kind of suretyship, not only because in that event he was excused from frankpledge, but also because there must

---

[1] Hudson (*Leet Jurisdiction in Norwich*, pp. lv, lix) finds that in Norwich there was a certain correspondence between tithing limits and parish limits, and concludes that the tithing, as well as the tithingman, was attached to a district. In Oxford and some other boroughs frankpledge grouping follows the wards of the town. See Rogers, *Oxford City Docs.*, 198; Bateson, *Records of Leicester*, ii. 2.

[2] Britton, i. 48; Fleta, 40.

[3] *Antiquity of the Leet*, 19.

[4] Bracton (fol. 124b, ii. 306) believed that this oath, which he appears to have found in the *Leges Edwardi*, was made in the view of frankpledge even in the age when the *Leges* were written.

[5] *Chron. Jocelini de Brakelonda* (Camden Soc.), 74; Maitland, *Court Baron*, 77, 101; *Plac. de Quo War.*, 35.

[6] *Mirror of Justices*, 41.

be a record as to who was responsible for producing him in case he committed a felony. Many times the lord of persons in mainpast had a view of frankpledge of his own, in which he exercised jurisdiction in the matter. A literal reading, however, of the rule requiring all to take oath in the view of frankpledge, considered in connection with the presentments concerning those in mainpast and those who had not taken the oath of fealty, leads to the inference that upon reaching the age of twelve,[1] or upon entering service under a new lord in a new community, these retainers not in the franchises of the county were required to attend the sheriff's view and to swear allegiance to the king, as well as abstinence from crime and from association with criminals.

A second variety of view of frankpledge is now to be considered, — that of the court leet, held not by the sheriff or his bailiffs but by a manorial steward as representative of a feudal lord. To the modern mind the plan of supervision through agents of the crown will appear adequate and statesmanlike. At first thought, therefore, it cannot but seem strange that a royal power, strong enough to enforce such a system, should have tolerated beside it one under which a private person was permitted in his own court to hold view of frankpledge. A feudal lord never was a private person to his dependents, however, for feudalism had a political as well as an economic side. Jurisdiction was a thing of value, and when feudalism was at its height any right or perquisite which brought a financial return was liable to enfeoffment. Moreover, there can hardly be a doubt that the right of inspecting frankpledge tithings, with the emoluments consequent to this right, had been in the hands of some members of the feudal nobility before Henry II created

---

[1] Britton (i. 48) says fourteen; but in this assertion he contradicts both himself and other writers.

what is properly known as view of frankpledge. The subject has thus a significance reaching much farther than the question as to view of frankpledge; for both in Bracton and in the quo warranto pleas the court leet appears as the typical franchise. The manner of its acquisition and exercise, therefore, tends to throw light on the other regalian rights which the lords enjoyed. ✐

The word leet is used, after the reign of Edward I,[1] to denote the complex of police jurisdictional powers which were associated in the sheriff's tourn and which embraced the view of frankpledge. Originally the leet was a territorial division of the hundred in East Anglia;[2] but, like other such divisions in England, it came in time to give its name to a court. The jurisdiction of this court in Norfolk and Suffolk so nearly corresponded to that of the tourn, — which lords all over England were claiming, and which Edward I by his great quo warranto was attempting to define and to have declared a regalian privilege, — that the name was quickly adopted by lawyers, and early in the fourteenth century was used throughout the country. It first appears in a national statute in 1353.[3] The name is thus synonymous with view of frankpledge in the technical sense, as well as with the view of the tithings and all the petty privileges that went with it. It is doubtless this ambiguity in the use of the old term that explains the sudden rise to popularity of the new one. Besides *leta*, the terms *visus franci plegii* and *curia cum visu franciplegii, visus de borchtrunung* [4] and *visus tethingorum*,[5] also occur as designations for this kind of court.

---

[1] It is used officially before the royal justices in 1292. See *Year Book*, 20–21 Edw. I, 297.

[2] Gage, *Suffolk*, pp. xii–xvii.

[3] Hearnshaw, *Leet Jurisdiction in England*, 14.

[4] Vinogradoff, *Villainage*, 363, note 1. In *Rot. Hundred.*, ii. 147 (Suffolk), *bortr'* is the form used.

[5] As in *Plac. de Quo War.*, 259.

In the later thirteenth century a valid exercise of the franchise known as view of frankpledge meant an exercise of the powers of the sheriff in the tourn. All the articles concerning which the sheriff made inquiry for the preservation of the peace were to be used. Not only was there actual view of the tithings, but presentments were also taken concerning treasure trove, thieves and other malefactors, the assize of bread and beer, roads obstructed, waters turned, hue raised, blood shed, false measures and weights, and the various other articles on the list.[1] View of frankpledge, argues the king's attorney in 1287, means that all of the age of twelve ought to appear in court twice a year for the conservation of the peace, and for making presentments in regard to all necessary articles to be reported at the eyre.[2] In 1330 a successor to this official declares that view of frankpledge is a royal liberty, which ought to be a unit in itself and which ought not to vary in particular cases; that it was instituted *ab initio* for the inquiry by capital pledges concerning all the articles touching this view.[3] So well, indeed, did view of frankpledge come to be known as a term to denote the leet jurisdiction that the phrase, with practically all that it connotes, is to be found in the fourteenth and succeeding centuries in Wales, and in various parts of England where frankpledge itself never existed.[4]

The process by which these powers were transferred from royal to seigniorial hands before their final grouping in the reign of Edward I was a long and necessarily a gradual one, dating in general from the reign of Henry II, but in some of its aspects existing long before his time. The oldest traceable phase is the

[1] See *Plac. de Quo War.*, 1, 3, 4, 5, 9.
[2] *Ibid.* 249.
[3] *Ibid.* 505.
[4] See above, pp. 44; 53, note 2. A cursory examination of Hearnshaw's list of modern courts leet (*Leet Jurisdiction*, 248-321) will sufficiently show this fact.

putting of men in *borh* in a private jurisdiction, a practice to be discovered as early as the Kentish laws of Athelstan. Canute's law seems to require that all be put in *borh* in the hundred, but even in his day some local jurisdictions were certainly outside the royal hundreds.[1] Grants of authority over hundreds, made by Edward the Confessor and William the Conqueror,[2] must have involved a right to put men in suretyship; and old Anglo-Saxon grants of *frithsoken* seem to have conferred the same right.[3] A conveyance, in the late Saxon and early Norman periods, of the privileges known as *sake* and *soke* probably had a similar effect; for in the first half of the twelfth century such grants certainly empowered magnates to punish in their own courts dependents of their mainpast whenever the hue was raised after them.[4] As late as 1268 the justices in eyre in Wiltshire assumed that this clause in a charter of Henry I had conferred the rights appurtenant to the view of frankpledge.[5] Such a decision would not have been made twenty years later, for the obvious reason that the courts of Edward I required specific mention of this franchise before they would recognize the validity of such a grant;[6] and specific mention earlier than the reign of Henry II could occur in no genuine charter.[7] But in what-

---

[1] See Maitland, *Domesday Book and Beyond*, 260–290.

[2] *Ibid.* 92, 260.

[3] Maitland, *Select Pleas in Manorial Courts*, p. xxiii, and note 3. A charter of Henry III in his thirty-seventh year explains a grant of *frithsoken* by Richard I to the monks of St. John, Colchester, as "view of frankpledge within their liberties" (*Rot. Chart.*, ed. Hardy, i. pt. i. p. xxxvii, note 1).

[4] *Leges Edw. Conf.*, xxi. 1, in Liebermann, *Gesetze*, i. 647.

[5] *Calendar of Charter Rolls*, ii. 93–94.

[6] "Non possit recedere de Corona domini regis nisi specialiter fiat mencio de eisdem libertatibus in carta ipsius domini regis." — *Plac. de Quo War.*, 432.

[7] It is absolutely certain, therefore, that thirteenth-century claims of view of frankpledge dating from the Conquest are not based on fact. When the justices at the time of the great quo warranto do admit such a claim from a charter

ever terms the right to put men in frankpledge had been granted by the king, or whether, as we may be practically certain for the reign of Stephen, it had been assumed as a feudal right, the wording of the Assize of Clarendon [1] clearly shows that this privilege, and surely with it the attendant police jurisdiction, had since the reign of Henry I been exercised in seigniorial courts from which the sheriff was excluded.

The period during which the lords acquired most of the privileges subsequently grouped together in the court leet was the century following 1166. It has already been observed that, when Henry II introduced the presentment jury into the sheriff's tourn in place of private appeal or of the mere report of capital pledges when questioned, the effectiveness of the new plan made police jurisdiction profitable. "Wholesale," says Maitland, "the feudal lords grasped at this new procedure; nor can the king and his officers have tried to resist them very seriously. On the whole it was for the good of the peace that there should be as much presenting of the offenders as was possible." [2] Not till the reign of Henry III does there appear evidence of any systematic attempt to resist such assumption, but the civil war and the confusion of the rest of the reign favored further usurpation. From the battle of Evesham seems to have dated the exercise of many an unauthorized liberty which Edward I sought to regain. Sometimes view of frankpledge was given over to a lord with the requirement that it be made in presence of the king's bailiff, and very often the exercise of the right was sanctioned by the king for a small annual payment; but in most cases it was merely a matter

prior to the time of Henry II, it is not because the franchise is specifically conveyed, but merely because the wording of the grant is so indefinite, or so incapable of definition at the time, that the conveyance of view of frankpledge cannot well be denied. See *Plac. de Quo War.*, 83, 92, 93, 254, 729.

[1] Ch. ix, in Stubbs, *Select Charters*, 144.

[2] *Select Pleas in Manorial Courts*, p. xxxvi.

of the unauthorized appropriation of a profitable right,[1] often with the connivance of the sheriff, as is clearly shown by the numerous cases of withdrawal of suit of tourn, even under Edward I. By his reign view of frankpledge seems to have been the most common of all the franchises in private hands.[2] So surprisingly numerous, indeed, are the instances of assumption of these privileges that Maitland was even led to doubt "whether in the past they had been regarded as *regalia*, and whether the act of assuming them had been regarded as wrongful." [3]

An attempt to maintain the rights of the crown in the view of frankpledge is evident before the development of the franchise begins. Henry II went so far as to declare that even in manorial courts view of frankpledge should be before the sheriff; [4] but he undoubtedly claimed more than he gained, and no doubt more than he hoped to gain. In some cases his charters acquit the grantee of suits and pleas in the hundred court,[5] a policy which enabled him to assume this jurisdiction himself; and some of these grants even forbid the sheriff or any other royal official to enter the hundred.[6] Although Henry no doubt regained many rights usurped during the reign of his weak predecessor, yet the quo warranto proceedings of a century later show too many lords holding view of frankpledge by prescription from the coronation of his successor to admit of the belief that he carried out his theory, or that he legalized these rights

---

[1] A grant of the privilege in specific terms had been quite unusual. Cf. Maitland, *Select Pleas in Manorial Courts*, pp. xxii, 86.

[2] Pollock and Maitland, *English Law* (1895), i. 557. An examination of the hundred and the quo warranto rolls quickly convinces one of the truth of the statement. See above, pp. 65–66.

[3] *Select Pleas in Manorial Courts*, p. xxi.

[4] Assize of Clarendon, ch. ix, in Stubbs, *Select Charters*, 144.

[5] Dugdale, *Monasticon*, iv. 515, vi. 64; *Plac. de Quo War.*, 251.

[6] *Chron. Monast. Abingdon* (Rolls Series), ii. 217, 235.

by special act, except in a very few cases. What he had really done was tacitly to recognize the feudal principle that customary possession of a franchise constituted lawful possession. The results of this policy his successors had to accept. The prudent Marshal in 1217 found it worth while to promise to the barons, angered into rebellion by John's violations of their customary rights, that the sheriff should make his view of frankpledge in such manner as to preserve to them intact the liberties which they possessed in the time of Henry II, as well as those subsequently acquired in rightful manner.[1] It would thus appear that John had deviated from the moderation of his father by attempting to carry out too literally the principle laid down in the Assize of Clarendon. An effort to check seigniorial usurpation was again apparent when in 1254 the justices at Lichfield made inquiry concerning those who, since the war between John and the barons, had withdrawn suit of shires or hundreds or sheriff's aids by leave of the sheriffs and bailiffs or by assent of the king; and still again when, in the next year, the justices were commissioned to inquire throughout the kingdom who held view of frankpledge without the sheriff and without warrant of the king.[2] Henry III was never able to follow up the matter. His great successor, however, continued to act along this line for no less than sixteen years, conducting a thorough inquest into regalian rights in private possession, and then, by the great quo warranto, systematically attacking unauthorized franchises. Finally, by his statute of 1290 he confirmed not only the policy of Henry II but also the very status of affairs which had existed during the latter's reign. Liberties used from a period before the time of King Richard without misuse were to

---

[1] Magna Carta of 1217, ch. xlii, *Statutes of the Realm*, i. 17–19; Stubbs, *Select Charters*, 346.

[2] *Annales Monastici* (Rolls Series), i. 331, 337, 338.

be confirmed by patent of the king, and other liberties were to be judged by the custom of the realm.[1]

The result of the quo warranto of Edward I, so far as it affected view of frankpledge, was a compromise. The franchise was left largely in the hands of those who already held it; but its regalian character was affirmed, and the royal right to fix the conditions under which it should be exercised, and thus to unify its procedure, was clearly established. Many of the wrongful holders of the franchise had long been in seisin; and juries were, out of mere ignorance, likely to swear that such seisin had been held since legal memory. It is interesting to note that, when in the earlier stages of the proceedings the royal attorneys set up the theory that view of frankpledge could "only be deduced from an *antecessor* who had come in with the Norman Conqueror," [2] the lords set about proving this utterly impossible duration of seisin, just as they later established it merely for a single century. The quo warranto pleas show that, out of a multitude of cases examined, the number of franchises actually assumed by the king was very small. In his son's reign there seems to have been a renewed usurpation of them, which was investigated in a new quo warranto at the beginning of the reign of Edward III, an examination which showed that, as a rule, a view of frankpledge forfeited to the king was restored on condition of a small annual payment.[3] By the fifteenth century view of frankpledge had come to be associated with the manorial court rather than with the sheriff's tourn, a judicial decision of 1441 even denying to the tourn the legal jurisdiction of the leet.[4] As to the number of views that

---

[1] *Statutes of the Realm*, i. 107.
[2] *Plac. de Quo War.*, 93, 434, 437.
[3] *Ibid.* 21, 31, 35, 36, 96, 161, 505, 508, 514–517, 536, 576.
[4] *Year Book*, 18 Hen. VI, Trin., pl. 11.

had fallen into private hands there is some hint in the explanation considered necessary by Sir Thomas Smith in the second half of the sixteenth century, wherein he sets forth that a court leet is not incident to every manor, but is acquired only by special grant or by long prescription.[1]

The uniformity of practice attained through the attack of Edward I on the franchises was, after all, the great result. In order to retain those rights which were now collectively known as leet jurisdiction, a lord must demonstrate that he had rightfully acquired them and had used them according to the custom of the realm. The authoritative criterion for determining this custom was, of course, to be sought in the royal jurisdiction of the tourn. The court leet remained in the hands of the lords; but from a seigniorial court it had come to be part of the national judicial system, which in less than a century Parliament was to regulate.[2] According to later English law, the power of the sheriff in the tourn and that of the steward in the leet are one.[3]

After 1290 the law required that the holder of view of frankpledge either must have a definite concession of this right from the crown or must inherit it from some one who did have such a concession.[4] It was no longer possible to claim that quittance of frankpledge or of suit of hundred, or some other vague expression in an old charter, conferred such a power.[5] Nor

---

[1] *The Common-welth of England*, 88 (80).

[2] In 1376. See *Rot. Parl.*, ii. 368.

[3] *Year Book*, 22 Edw. IV, Mich., pl. 2; Powell, *Antiquity of the Leet*, 22. Of a statute concerning the tourn, Coke says, "This tourn of the sheriff is *Curia Vicecomitis Franciplegii* (as it hath been said) and therefore this act extended to all leets and views of frankpledge of all other lords and persons " (comment on the Statute of Marlborough, ch. x, in his *Second Institute*, 1671, p. 121).

[4] In the hundred of Calne in 1255 Eva de Cantilupe held view of frankpledge as part of her widow's third. See *Rot. Hundred.*, ii. 230, 236, 239; Marsh, *Calne*, 24.

[5] Pollock and Maitland, *English Law* (1895), i. 560, note 1; *Plac. de Quo War.*, 83, 92, 93.

could view of frankpledge any longer pass by simple enfeoffment.[1] Even a grant of Richard I conferring "all liberties
which the crown can confer" was in 1331 rejected by the king's
justices as not containing specific reference to view of frankpledge.[2]

To retain his view of frankpledge in the age of Edward I the
lord had to conform to minute regulations as to the manner in
which he used it. The king's attorneys made a determined
effort to prevent the exercise of such jurisdiction over detached
pieces of land, on the ground that presentments for conserving
the peace ought to be made by neighbors. Since, according
to the custom of the realm, the presentment jury had to consist
of twelve men, and since in the private view of frankpledge these
twelve were capital pledges, it followed, according to the royal
theory, that the lord must have twelve tithings. The presentors,
moreover, must all live in the same county, for the sheriff could
hold view of frankpledge in his own county only. These theories, however, prevailed only in part. View of frankpledge
was sometimes held, without any protest from the king's officers,
not only for men on very small tracts of land,[3] but for those on
detached areas as well.[4]

Within the precincts of his leet the lord was expected, in the
time of Edward I, assiduously to exercise the liberties which he
claimed, at the same time taking care that he did not do that
which was contrary to custom or that for which he had no war-

---

[1] *Plac. de Quo War.*, 4, 10; Salt Archaeol. Soc., *Collections*, vi. pt. i. 243;
Calendar of Charter Rolls, ii. 93–94.

[2] *Plac. de Quo War.*, 15–16.

[3] In Cambridgeshire it is to be found on two carucates of land, and in another
case on a knight's fee, which had twenty-three acres of arable and six acres of
wood. In still another instance, a view of frankpledge went with the gift of one
hide of land, though it no doubt was held for men on other hides as well. See
Rot. Hundred., ii. 552, 556, 710.

[4] Pollock and Maitland, *English Law* (1895), i. 568.

rant. The grant of view of frankpledge made to him was, according to Bracton, valid only when exercised.[1] If a lord whose view included the duty of hanging thieves let his gallows fall down, he thereby lost the liberty,[2] as he did also if he claimed the right to punish infractions of the assize of bread and beer and did not maintain a pillory and tumbril for the purpose.[3] If he did not hold his view regularly, or if he let a session of the eyre pass without making a formal claim to the franchise which he held, either fact might be cited in evidence against him if his right was questioned.[4] Likewise, if he once made the usual payment to the sheriff for holding view, this circumstance was evidence against him, for the king was in seisin of such payment.[5] On the other hand, he must be careful not to assume jurisdiction wrongfully. If without special arrangement he held view in the absence of the king's bailiff, he lost the privilege.[6] If he had his capital pledge make inquiry concerning other articles than those which he claimed,[7] or if he took presentments on the articles of purpresture and the assize of bread and beer made by the reeve with less than four men,[8] he forfeited his view. Above all, at the end of the thirteenth and the beginning of the fourteenth century, he must not without a special grant punish delinquencies in the last-named matter by substituting amercement for the pillory and tumbril;[9] for the taking of fines in such cases was so serious an infringement of the prerogative of the king that it was a sure ground for the forfeiture of the view.[10]

As the private view of frankpledge was a substitute for the

---

[1] Bracton, fol. 56, i.
[2] *Plac. de Quo War.*, 303.
[3] *Ibid.* 34.
[4] *Ibid.* 19, 33.
[5] *Ibid.* 88.
[6] *Ibid.* 65.
[7] *Ibid.* 35, 42–43.
[8] *Ibid.* 604–605.
[9] See *Calendar of Patent Rolls*, Edw. I, 1272–1281, p. 418.
[10] See, for example, *Plac. de Quo War.*, 31–36, 516.

tourn, its sessions had to be held ordinarily at the same period and practically at the same date twice a year, at Martinmas and Hokeday.[1] This was true as early as 1225,[2] and probably as early as 1166. Since by the Great Charter of 1217 the sheriff was to make view of frankpledge at but one tourn each year, some of the lords were not slow to seize upon this parallel as an excuse for holding but one leet each year in their courts. The claim that but one view had been customary was very likely to be made when a fief with view passed from the hands of the king to those of one of his subjects. As early as 1234, however, the King's Bench held technically that the two tourns of the sheriff each year were views of frankpledge.[3] In the time of Edward I there was complaint that the Templars made view of frankpledge twice where the king, according to the custom of the county, made it but once;[4] but the royal attorney, holding to the theory that a tourn was a view of frankpledge, declared that the holding of view once a year was "against the custom of the realm and the form of the Great Charter."[5] Sometimes, however, it is shown that view was actually made but once a year.[6] At the beginning of the reign of Edward III a lord might for an annual payment be allowed to choose his own time for holding this yearly session.[7]

It was the policy of the Plantagenets, following the decree of Henry II, to have view of frankpledge in manorial courts made in presence of the sheriff or of his bailiff whenever possible. To use the phrase of the royal attorney, the bailiff was to come and

---

[1] In *Rot. Hundred.*, i. 101, there is reference to the tourn's being held at these two dates. Hokeday was the second Sunday after Easter.

[2] *Cart. St. Peter of Gloucester* (Rolls Series), ii. 36, 182.

[3] *Bracton's Note Book*, ii. 401–402.

[4] *Rot. Hundred.*, i. 287 (Lincoln).

[5] *Plac. de Quo War.*, 299 (Huntingdon, 14 Edw. I).

[6] *Ibid.* 4 (Bedford, 5 Edw. I).

[7] *Ibid.* 50.

see that it was reasonably done.[1] Some of John's charters
specifically provide that view shall be made in presence of his
officer;[2] and one of the year 1202 grants view of frankpledge
to the abbot of Ramsey on all his lands, subject to the oversight
of the royal bailiff "according to the custom of the realm."[3]
This view was actually held, however, by the abbot's steward or
by his bailiffs.[4] On these manors, as elsewhere, the custom was
to give the royal bailiff reasonable summons, and then, if he did
not come, to hold court without him.[5] When one prelate turned
his view over to another he sometimes made a similar provision
for supervision by his own officers.[6] Henry III and Edward I
both made to prelates grants of view of frankpledge which ordinarily excluded the royal officials;[7] but, although in such instances the king's representative had no right to attend, it was a
special privilege to be allowed to hold these sessions in his absence.[8] For doing so without leave no less distinguished a
person than Earl Humphrey Bohun forfeited his view of frankpledge on some of his estates in Huntingdonshire.[9] The object
of the king's insistence on this point was to gain recognition of
his ultimate right of control. Bracton says that, although in
general the king's sheriffs and bailiffs are to be prohibited from
entering any one's estate upon a liberty granted by the king,
nevertheless by virtue of the gift of the liberty they may in the

---

[1] *Plac. de Quo War.*, 104.

[2] Such a charter to the Bishop of Sarum in 1200 is to be found in the *Register
of St. Osmund* (Rolls Series), i. 211.

[3] *Ramsey Chartulary* (Rolls Series), ii. 63.

[4] *Ibid.* i. 285, 286, 295, 343, 355, 491.

[5] *Plac. de Quo War.*, 104.

[6] *Ramsey Chartulary*, ii. 321.

[7] *Calendar of Charter Rolls*, ii. 142, 331, 485–486. A confirmation of such a
grant to the abbot of Peterborough included eight hundreds in Northamptonshire.

[8] *Plac. de Quo War.*, 245, 293.

[9] *Ibid.* 303.

king's name make summons and attachments and views of frankpledge and all things pertaining to the crown.[1] Even in a charter of Edward excluding his officials from the land of the prioress of Ambresbury the right of entry in cases of default is reserved.[2] After this principle gained recognition it seems to have been customary to leave the view of frankpledge completely in the hands of the manorial steward, under the operation of the rule, to be found still in force at a much later time, that, if the steward did not properly discharge his duty toward the public peace, the sheriff or the justices in eyre might take presentments in his stead.[3]

At the manorial view of frankpledge, as at the sheriff's view, the attendance of peasants was required in person and not merely by reason of tenure.[4] It was the duty of the manorial steward to see that the bailiffs were warned to summon to court for the time appointed those who owed suit.[5] In the thirteenth and fourteenth centuries it was customary for the lord to specify suit at the semiannual views of frankpledge as one of the conditions upon which his tenants held their land of him;[6] but whether or not they owed such suit without a direct bargain seems to have depended upon custom.[7] Certain classes of the

---

[1] Fol. 56b, i. 448.

[2] *Calendar of Charter Rolls*, ii. 351.

[3] *Year Book*, 10 Hen. IV, Mich., pl. 9.

[4] *Ibid.* 21–22 Edw. I, 399.

[5] Maitland, *Court Baron*, 69.

[6] See, for example, *Cart. St. Peter of Gloucester* (Rolls Series), ii. 251; *Inquisitiones post Mortem for Wiltshire* (Wiltshire Archaeol. and Nat. Hist. Soc.), pt. iii. 184; Willis-Bund, *Inquisitiones post Mortem for Worcester* (Worcestersh. Hist. Soc.), pt. i. 29. It was expected by the abbot of Ramsey in 1219 that the holder of a hide of his land was to come with his tenants to the view of frankpledge, and was to pay two shillings once a year for each of those in tithing who did not come. See *Ramsey Chartulary*, i. 491.

[7] See Baigent, *Crondal Records* (Hampshire Record Soc.), pt. i. 13–14, 48; *Plac. de Quo War.*, 612; Willis-Bund, *Inquisitiones post Mortem for Worcester*, pt. i. 29.

unfree were not compelled to be present. Not only women and children but also personal attendants of the lord were excused; and special exemptions were made by the lord for shepherds, plough-boys, and men engaged in the carting service.[1] Moreover, as in the sheriff's view, it was usual to excuse from attendance the great body of men in frankpledge (but often for a money payment), and to permit the tithing to appear by the capital pledge alone.[2] Such representation of a vill by its capital pledge at the semiannual law hundreds is recorded as early as 1227.[3]

The general procedure of view in the leet was necessarily the same as that in the tourn. The articles of view of frankpledge had to be the same in both courts, and after the latter part of the fourteenth century were subject to parliamentary regulation.[4] The jurors who made the presentments were, however, much more likely to be capital pledges than in the sheriff's view, for it was already the theory of the law in the time of Henry III that a lord could not put free men on oath without the direction of the king.[5] Presentment by villains, it is true, violated the principle that a free man was not to be indicted by one who was not free; but if it was necessary, as it seems to have been in some instances, for a sheriff to ignore this principle in order to get presentments at all, much more was it necessary for the manorial steward. Sometimes he was able to make inquest upon the oaths of twelve free tenants "charged upon the presentments of the frankpledges" after the fashion in the tourn; but more often, in spite of all complaint about the irregularity of allowing the head of a tithing to make presentments involving a free man,[6]

---

[1] Vinogradoff, *Villainage*, 363, and note 6.
[2] Pollock and Maitland, *English Law* (1895), i. 557.
[3] *Bracton's Note Book*, ii. 195.
[4] *Rot. Parl.*, ii. 368.
[5] *Rot. Hundred.*, ii. 203.
[6] *Ibid.* i. 442, ii. 203.

10

the leet jury consisted of twelve capital pledges.[1] It is only in rare instances that the empanelling of a leet jury is mentioned.[2] By 1340 the rule was laid down for the guidance of manorial stewards that, if there were not twelve free tenants, the presentments might be made by six bondmen and six freemen;[3] and by 1367 it was customary for them to be made by the chief pledges.[4] Maitland has even called attention to an admission by a judge in the time of Edward III to the effect that in some districts the articles of view were presented by twelve dozeners, in others by only two or three, "according to the usage of the country."[5] In 1405, however, the rule is clearly enunciated that presentments in the leet shall be by twelve and not fewer, otherwise they are traversable.[6] In some places double presentment by both jurors and heads of tithings was preserved. Sometimes presentments were offered to the jurors by representatives of four townships,[7] and sometimes by individual capital pledges, either without their tithings [8] or with them. Presentment at the manorial view of frankpledge was thus often made by the entire homage. In the south of England especially, but by no means exclusively there, it was usual for each tithingman to make presentments to the jurors, who then declared upon oath whether or not all the tithingmen had "presented well and faithfully in all things."[9]

---

[1] As in Maitland, *Court Baron*, 73, 87, 100, 110.

[2] As in Mayo, *Records of Shaftesbury*, 20.

[3] Maitland, *Court Baron*, 97.

[4] *Year Book*, 41 Edw. III, fol. 26, Mich., pl. 23.

[5] *Select Pleas in Manorial Courts*, p. xxxv.

[6] *Year Book*, 6 Hen. IV, Hillary, pl. 4.

[7] Maitland, *Court Baron*, 73.

[8] *Ibid.* 97; *Select Pleas in Manorial Courts*, 165, 168–169; Young, *Dulwich College*, ii. 282; Kitchin, *Manor of Manydown* (Hampshire Record Soc.), 134–135.

[9] Hone, *The Manor and Manorial Records*, 156; Maitland, *Select Pleas in Manorial Courts*, p. xxxiv.

Preservation of the peace and desire for the revenues consequent thereto were not the only motives that a lord had for
maintaining frankpledge. When a man was put in tithing in a
leet, his oath included, in some cases at any rate, not only the
usual pledge of fealty to the king, but also a special promise of
fealty to the lord, and sometimes of obedience to his bailiffs.[1]
Before the middle of the thirteenth century the reception of a
man into a tithing is thus connected with his reception into the
lord's service. Failure to be in the tithing might be a cause for
forfeiture of the land held of the lord.[2] The stranger, and in
the fourteenth century the boy who had reached the age of
twelve, were forbidden to remain on the lord's land unless they
were in tithing;[3] and whoever harbored the latter or let a
house to the former while this requirement was unfulfilled was
subject to an amercement. But there was yet another way in
which the tithing of the king served the ends of the lord. The
reading of the tithing-lists, and the presentment by the capital
pledges twice a year as to whether any were missing from their
tithings, revealed which of the villains were away from the
manor,[4] and enabled the steward to take measures in the leet to
secure their return.[5] Thus the maintenance of frankpledge by
the leet not only aided in the preservation of the king's peace
but also served purely manorial ends.

A second species of court leet to be noticed is that held in
boroughs where frankpledge existed. This was one of the most
important courts of the borough. Its beginnings are to be sought
as early as the decree of Henry II that men should not be received into boroughs and cities except under mainpast or in

---

[1] Maitland, *Court Baron*, 77, 101; Hone, *The Manor*, etc., 148.
[2] Baigent, *Crondal Records* (Hampshire Record Soc.), pt. i. 147.
[3] Maitland, *Court Baron*, 72, 97.
[4] *Ibid.* 69, 71, 72.
[5] Maitland, *Select Pleas in Manorial Courts*, 89, 168.

frankpledge;[1] and by 1473 it existed in most of the important towns and boroughs in England.[2] Before the time of Edward I it was sometimes held by prescription without royal concession, just as in the case of the manorial leet.[3] The semiannual view of frankpledge for the borough is often mentioned;[4] and one sometimes finds the statement that it was held near Michaelmas and Hokeday.[5] In some boroughs, however, as in some manors, the leet met but once a year. That at Southampton was, and still is, held on Hoke Tuesday.[6] At Ipswich in the thirteenth century, probably in accord with a local custom prevalent before 1200, view of frankpledge was held throughout the week of Pentecost.[7] Although such variety of practice undoubtedly often resulted from old local usage, in some cases it probably came from a like variety in manorial custom; for in numerous boroughs of the thirteenth and fourteenth centuries view of frankpledge was still in the hands of feudal overlords.[8] The

---

[1] Assize of Clarendon, ch. x, in Stubbs, *Select Charters*, 144.

[2] *Statutes of the Realm*, ii. 442.

[3] See above, p. 61, note 5.

[4] Griffith, *Records of Huntingdon*, 20; *Plac. de Quo War.*, 246 (Tewkesbury), 660 (Newark); Ogle, *Royal Letters to Oxford*, 35.

[5] Harrod, *Court Rolls of Colchester*, 8; Mayo, *Records of Shaftesbury*, 19.

[6] *Southampton Leet Records* (ed. Hearnshaw), i. p. xi.

[7] *Black Book of the Admiralty* (Rolls Series), ii. 130. Purprestures were to be removed by bailiffs and *chefs plegges presentours* within forty days afterwards.

[8] Thus in 1255 Eva de Cantilupe had a third part of the view in the borough of Calne as portion of her dower, her husband having had view for the whole hundred (*Rot. Hundred.*, ii. 236; Marsh, *Calne*, 24). In 1287 the abbot of Tewkesbury had a third interest in the view of the vill of Tewkesbury, and held the whole view in Bristol *extra portam Laffordi* (*Plac. de Quo War.*, 246). About the same time the bailiff of Earl Richard of Cornwall had view of the borough of Wycombe (*Rot. Hundred.*, i. 34). At Newark, where in 1330 the bishop of Lincoln claimed view of the half wapentake, his free burghers of the vill were required to come to the view but once a year (*Plac. de Quo War.*, 660). A similar exercise of power over the territory on which a borough was located is found in the south of England, Henry III having by charter granted to a certain Walter view of frankpledge on the lands of Guildford, both in the borough and out of it (*ibid.* 743).

tourn, moreover, which, as has been seen, sometimes served as a precedent for the practice of holding a manorial leet but once a year, not improbably influenced some of the boroughs in the same way. In a borough like Tavistock, for example, where before the king's charter was granted the sheriff made his tourn but once a year,[1] there might well have been a tendency to continue the same arrangement under the charter.

In towns that held their own view one of two general plans was followed. Either a view was held for the whole borough by the mayor and bailiffs or by the mayor and aldermen,[2] or else there were several wards or leets, each with its own view held by the alderman of the ward or by the bailiffs of the town. A typical example of the *mickletorn* occurs at Nottingham,[3] one of the sub-leet system at Norwich, while instances of the division of the tourn into wards, each in charge of an alderman, are found at Oxford[4] and London.[5] At Norwich, following the East Anglian plan of dividing the hundred into twelve leets, there seem to have been originally four great leets, each with three subdivisions, the sub-leets containing collectively about a hundred and sixty tithings, which were so distributed as all to fall within the body of one of the forty-six parishes.[6] In a borough in which the ward system of maintaining frankpledge was in vogue there were usually four wards.

As to what went on at these courts, town records occasionally give some information. In some of them there was the presentment of purprestures;[7] in others it was customary to make

---

[1] *Rot. Hundred.*, i. 81.
[2] Hedges, *Wallingford*, ii. 11; Davies, *Southampton*, 233.
[3] Stevenson, *Records of Nottingham*, i. 315.
[4] Rogers, *Oxford City Docs.*, 195, 197.
[5] *Liber Albus* (ed. Riley), i. 99.
[6] Hudson, *Leet Jurisdiction in Norwich*, p. liv.
[7] *Black Book of the Admiralty*, ii. 131.

inquiry concerning all the articles which the sheriff might use in his tourn.[1] At Ipswich in the thirteenth century and at Nottingham in the early fourteenth the presentors were capital pledges,[2] as they were also at a later time in towns of East Anglia and the north midlands.[3] At other places, both in the late thirteenth century and long afterwards, the burghers answered at the view, not by capital pledges, but by a jury of twelve,[4] which was empanelled. In boroughs capital pledges did not, it seems, usually present hue levied and blood shed, for in most places there were special officers to do this.[5] At Bury St. Edmunds, in 1198, it was already customary to keep rolls for recording the pledges, and to require the payment of the pence called *borth-selver* from those whose names were thus enrolled.[6] For London there is preserved a copy in French of an oath that was used in putting men in frankpledge;[7] and for Leicester an account of the pence received from some three hundred persons in tithing in the year 1375, and from a somewhat smaller number in 1376.[8] Such occasional glimpses of the borough leet in action reveal a procedure for presenting offences and for putting men in frankpledge like that of its manorial original.

[1] Harland, *Mamecestre* (Chetham Soc.), i. 194; Griffith, *Records of Huntingdon*, 20.

[2] *Black Book of the Admiralty*, ii. 131; Stevenson, *Records of Nottingham*, i. 66.

[3] Hudson, *Leet Jurisdiction in Norwich*, p. lxix; Cox and Markham, *Records of Northampton*, ii. 141.

[4] *Plac. de Quo War.*, 246.

[5] Maitland, *Court Baron*, 80.

[6] *Chron. Jocelini de Brakelonda* (Camden Soc.), 74.

[7] See Appendix B, below.

[8] Bateson, *Records of Leicester*, ii. 153.

CHAPTER V

DECLINE AND RESULTS OF THE FRANKPLEDGE SYSTEM

THE decline of frankpledge as an effective agency for keeping the peace of the realm dates from the very period in which the complete centralization of the machinery for its maintenance was achieved. The effort of the king to control the procedure of the leet system seems to have been due in part to a failure of the suretyship of the tithing and the presentments of the tithingman to secure a proper observance of the peace, and to his consequent desire to direct the leet as well as the tourn in such a manner as to correct this defect. The rule that the lord must in his view of frankpledge make inquiry concerning all the articles of the sheriff's tourn, taken with the rule that presentments must be made in a manner which the king's justices would recognize as valid, clearly reveals the royal purpose in this regard.

The failure of frankpledge to fulfill the prime object of its existence was obvious while Edward I was still on the throne. All over England crime seems to have been increasing. Gaol-delivery records show an unusually bad state of affairs. The preamble of the Statute of Winchester in 1285 complains of the wretched observance of the peace,[1] and the complaint is renewed in the *Articuli supra Cartas* fifteen years later.[2] In the year

[1] *Statutes of the Realm*, i. 96; Stubbs, *Select Charters*, 470.
[2] *Statutes of the Realm*, i. 154.

1285 the story of crime in the single hundred of North Erpingham in Norfolk is declared to be "so ghastly as positively to
stagger one ";[1] but much of this crime was committed by vag-
abonds, for whom no tithing could be responsible.[2]

The system of frankpledge had clearly lost its old effectiveness both in preventing crime and in securing the punishment
of criminals, a failure due partly to an antiquated system and
partly to a faulty mode of holding criminal courts. The tithingman was coming to act instead of the tithing in making
arrests and in offering presentments; and the ordinary members of the tithing, already often excused from actual appearance in tourn and leet, were thus being farther and farther
separated from direct touch with the police and criminal administration. To bring home to each locality a realizing sense of
its responsibility, therefore, Edward I enacted a new law making the people of each hundred and franchise responsible for
robberies and damages arising through their failure to produce
the offenders.[3] The half-mark usually paid by the tithing for
the escape of an offending member in the time of Henry II, —
so heavy a burden that in some instances the sheriff seems to
have been compelled to defer its collection for a year or even
longer,[4] — had now come to represent a far slighter value, the
payment of which was inadequate to spur the community to
capture a fugitive neighbor with whom it was often in sym-
pathy. The actual sum collected, moreover, in the reign of
Edward I, as well as in the reigns of his son and grandson, was

---

[1] Jessopp, *Coming of the Friars*, 100; Rye, in *Archaeol. Review*, ii. 206 ff.

[2] Thus, Assize Roll, No. 12 (Public Record Office), containing a record of the
Bedford eyre, 15 Edward I, shows that in practically every serious case the
criminal is either *vagabundus* or *alienus extraneus*. The other assize rolls of the
time show a similar increase of itinerancy on the part of criminals.

[3] Statute of Winchester, ch. i, *Statutes of the Realm*, i. 96; Stubbs, *Select
Charters*, 470.

[4] Compare *Pipe Roll*, 12 Hen. II, 14, 70, with *Pipe Roll*, 13 Hen. II, 106, 161.

often but forty pence, just half the original amount.[1] By the
end of the thirteenth century the clumsy plan of utilizing the
frankpledge tithing as constabulary had, in short, become ob-
scured by the many other functions thrust upon it, by the
appointment of special peace officers, and by the frequent performance of this particular service, as well as of the other
duties of the tithing, by the one man who was fast coming
to represent the activity of the whole group. That the employment of special officers rather than groups of men was a more
effective provision for conserving the peace the legislation
of Edward I clearly shows.

Furthermore, even when the tithing had arrested an offending member, delivered him up, and duly made presentment of
his offence, justice was in many cases far from being speedily
meted out to him. In local matters punishable in the leet, such
as infraction of the assize of bread and beer, the payment of a
small semiannual amercement really served as a license; and
in more serious cases there was undoubtedly a corresponding
miscarriage of justice. In the time of Henry III the eyres of
the justices were so infrequent that persons indicted before the
sheriff for grave crimes were likely to die or to escape before
they were brought to trial. When in this reign it became
customary to hold an eyre in a given county no oftener than
once in seven years, the amercement of a tithing for failure to
do its duty often became a mere form; for the body that was
fined might well be made up of altogether different persons
from those who had defaulted several years before. To remedy
this defect, Edward I developed the plan of sending out justices
of assize under special commissions, without waiting for the
long period of the eyre to come round; but even this plan was

---

[1] Assize Rolls, No. 11, mm. 23, 23*b* (Bedford, 15 Edw. I); No. 926, mm. 34,
34*b* (Sussex, 6 Edw. I).

still inadequate. Then for a time special commissions were issued to justices of *trailbaston* to try offenders,[1] an experiment which may be taken as showing the failure of the tourn system[2] and the search for a more efficient mode of restraining and punishing criminal impulses. After various laws had been passed in the course of another half-century, — among them one in 1340 attempting to secure more competent bailiffs in all hundreds,[3] and another in 1350 requiring local justices to make sessions in all counties four times a year to enforce the Statute of Labourers,[4] — it was finally in 1360 decided to try the plan of making three or four such justices in each county direct commissioners of the crown with power to hear all cases of felony and misdemeanor.[5] According to a statute of 1362, these "justices of the peace and of labourers" were to make sessions four times a year.[6] Thus was established a system of bringing to trial offenders against the peace which proved so efficient that, with some changes in 1387, and especially some in 1415, it has been followed down to the present time.[7]

These quarterly sessions in each county soon sapped what vitality remained in frankpledge. So long as presentments of ordinary offences were made chiefly by the capital pledges in the tourn and the leet, it was necessary at least to go through the form of putting men in tithings that there might be capital pledges; but, when the peace might be maintained through courts held by special royal commissioners without any neces-

---

[1] *Parl. Writs*, i. 407; *Rot. Parl.*, i. 128.

[2] Nichols, in *Archaeologia*, xl. pt. i. 94, 100.

[3] *Statutes of the Realm*, i. 284.

[4] *Ibid.* 313.

[5] *Ibid.* 365; Beard, *Office of Justice of the Peace*, 35–44; Howard, *Development of the King's Peace*, 37–41.

[6] *Statutes of the Realm*, i. 374.

[7] Cox, *Derbyshire*, i. 1.

sary attachment to the older local methods of the tourn,[1] the
capital pledge, with whom the duty of prosecuting crime had
mainly rested, declined in importance. By 1415 the justices of
the peace had gained preference over the sheriff as agents of
the crown in making inquiry concerning crown interests;[2] and
by 1461 the sheriff was by a well-known statute of that year
required to bring all presentments made in his tourn before the
justices at their next session, and was even forbidden to make
arrests on such presentments without process from the justices.[3]
As the new jurisdiction gained at the expense of the older one,
the heads of tithings tended to lose their national significance
and to retain importance in local matters only. The decline of
double presentment at the tourn in its later days seems to show
that even here the jury of twelve freemen had come to assume
entire charge of affairs,[4] and hence that the aid of twelve capital
pledges was no longer required. Such also was the effect of
creating county governments in some of the boroughs, and of
holding tourns in which the sheriff appointed the jurors.[5]

As a surety system, frankpledge declined rapidly in the fourteenth century. Not only did a dependence upon constables
and tithingmen to make arrests and lead offenders to prison
tend to free the tithing from its old duty of producing its members for trial, but the practice of substituting for the justices in
eyre commissions of gaol delivery, *oyer* and *terminer*, and
justices of the peace displaced the old-time medium through
which was collected from the tithing the now nominal payment
for failure to perform such service. It was at the eyre that presentment used to be made as to the tithing to which a fugitive

---

[1] See Bacon, *Government of England*, 302.
[2] *Rot. Parl.*, iv. 69.
[3] *Statutes of the Realm*, ii. 390–391.
[4] Maitland, *Select Pleas in Manorial Courts*, p. xxxiv.
[5] Hudson, *Leet Jurisdiction in Norwich*, pp. lxxix, lxxx.

belonged; but the records of proceedings before the new commissioners sent out by Edward I show these officers going straight to the merits of the cases which they tried. Never is there the slightest hint of an attempt to hold a tithing responsible for a flight. Even before the era of the quarter sessions begins it is evident that the maintenance of tithings is really a manorial and not a national affair. As the peasants purchased exemption from their other servile burdens or secured commutation of them, it was no longer possible to hold them to the ancient obligations of the tithing. In a late eyre for Northampton, held in 1330, there still appears the old form of holding tithings responsible for fugitive members;[1] but at least as early as 1337 a man was able to gain exemption from frankpledge by paying the lord of the manor a money fine.[2] In assize rolls of the fifteenth century, which two centuries earlier would have been sure to mention pledging by the tithings, there is no reference to the subject; and more significant still is a decision by the King's Bench in 1441, which says that the court leet has cognizance of several articles (such as amends of the assize of bread and beer) not included in the jurisdiction of the sheriff's tourn.[3] This removal of well-known articles of view of frankpledge from the dominion of the tourn is interpreted by no less eminent an authority than Fitzherbert as a ruling that the sheriff is not to receive presentments of those out of tithing.[4] It seems almost certain, therefore, that before the end of the fourteenth century men were no longer put in tithing in the tourn. By 1497 even Chief-justice Fineux of the King's Bench knew nothing of the former significance of frankpledge.[5]

[1] Public Record Office, Assize Roll, No. 632.
[2] Clark, in *Eng. Hist. Review*, xix. 717.
[3] *Year Book*, 18 Hen. VI, Trin., pl. 1.
[4] *La Graunde Abridgement*, pt. iii. fol. 90.
[5] *Year Book*, 12 Hen. VII, fol. 18. See *Manchester Leet Records* (Chetham

The disappearance of the surety element in the frankpledge system by no means prevented more or less observance of its forms for centuries more. To declare, as Marquardsen does,[1] that in the time of Henry VI and Edward IV "the last traces of frankpledge vanish from English law," is going too far. Powell, in the seventeenth century, would say only that the ancient obligation of every person above the age of twelve to have a pledge "by desuetude of time is utterly antiquated "; but some of the old functions of the view of frankpledge he recognized as still in existence.[2] At an earlier time Lambard even argued in favor of restoring to the tithingman his ancient functions, and knew no reason why, according to the law as it stood, such a plan might not be carried out.[3] After the fifteenth century tithings were still maintained both in boroughs and in manorial leets. The tithing-list, and the presentment of the capital pledges upon the articles of the view of frankpledge, were as useful as ever for registering the names of residents, and for keeping account of persons who left the jurisdiction, as well as of those newly arrived. The presentment of offences by the capital pledges was always convenient, and was even necessary for the maintenance of the leet when there were not twelve free jurors within its precincts. Such a continuance of the old frankpledge organization was also useful to the general government, in that it helped to keep the peace, provided tithingmen to serve as petty constables in the leet as well as under the jurisdiction of the justices of the peace, and preserved the medium through which the peasantry were sworn to the king's allegiance. Moreover, it would appear that the justices of the peace sometimes made use

---

Soc.), prefatory chapter, p. 7, where Fineux's statements are actually accepted as authority.

[1] Marquardsen, *Haft*, 70.

[2] Powell, *Antiquity of the Leet*, 18.

[3] Lambard, *Constables*, 9.

of the presentments of the capital pledges; for even at the
beginning of the seventeenth century the local constable —
who was but the lineal successor of the old head of the tithing,
and was still called borsholder, tithingman, or headbourow [1] —
was bound either to attend quarter sessions or to pay a fine, and
had the right to present anything that in his opinion demanded
the attention of the court.[2] Practical utility thus combined with
British conservatism to keep alive parts of a defunct organism.

Many survivals of the frankpledge system are to be found in
England as late as the nineteenth century. When in the fifteenth century it ceased to be customary to enroll men in separate tithings for the same manor, the peasants belonging to
the rural leet and to the lower classes in the borough leet were
entered by name upon a roll, and by taking the oath of fealty
were sworn into this "tithing of the lord king." [3] Such a swearing and enrolment of those above the age of twelve was continued as late as the seventeenth century.[4] This practice facili-
tated the tracing of vagrants and of suspected and undesirable
persons, and the exclusion of them from a community; for no
person was allowed to remain more than a year in a place unless he were sworn in court and had his name entered upon the
court rolls. In the seventeenth century such a formal reception
of men in ward was revived in London as a means of detecting

---

[1] Lambard, *Constables*, 9.

[2] Willis-Bund, *Quarter Sessions Rolls* (Worcestersh. Hist. Soc.), i. 133, ii.
p. xcviii; Cox, *Derbyshire*, i. 104; Atkinson, *Quarter Sessions Records* (North
Riding Record Soc.), i. 200. Powell (*Antiquity of the Leet*, 17), speaking from
the standpoint of his time, represents presentments in the tourn and leet as
originally made by constables and petty constables.

[3] Young, *Dulwich College*, ii. 281, 282; Maurer, *Saxon Mark Courts*, 34;
L. T. Smith, *Common-place Book*, 160.

[4] Powell, *Antiquity of the Leet*, 19. In Kitchin's *Le Court Leete*, fol. 51, men
are fined for living within the precinct of a view of frankpledge for a year without taking the oath of allegiance to the queen.

religious dissenters,[1] and those sworn were said to be in frankpledge. By the early part of this century the swearing into the
king's obedience of the young men and youths who had lived
in the town a year and a day had been discontinued in Southampton, a circumstance which the leet jury complained of in
1615, but did nothing farther about than to refer the matter
to the steward of the court.[2] The making of burgesses in the
leet courts, in this century and the early part of the next one,[3]
answered a purpose similar to that of receiving men into manorial tithings.

Even more persistent than enrolment in tithing was the election of capital pledges. From the first years of the fifteenth
century to the last years of the seventeenth, it is possible to
trace in the same court leet the appointment of these minor
officials in the same way and their performance of practically
the same duties.[4] The man who after his election to the office
of headbourow in 1660 refused to be sworn was fined just as
was his predecessor at the head of a tithing three centuries
earlier, only he was fined several times as heavily.[5] In parts
of Derbyshire in the fifteenth and sixteenth centuries there were
elected for each township at annual courts leet one or more
presentment jurors, usually from two to six, who collectively
were called the frankpledge.[6] In the reign of Henry VII the
tithingmen of eight tithings of the stannary of Blackmore appeared with their tithings in the hundred of Powder to do suit
and to present criminals.[7] The heads of tithings, who in the

---

[1] Stow, *Survey of London*, 671.
[2] Davies, *Southampton*, 234.
[3] Griffith, *Records of Huntingdon*, 49.
[4] Young, *Dulwich College*, ii. 281–320.
[5] *Ibid.* 317.
[6] Yeatman, *Feudal History of Derby*, § vi. 340–389, 429.
[7] Public Record Office, Court Rolls of Stannaries, Bundle 157, No. 13.

reign of Edward I served virtually as petty constables, from the time of Edward III served regularly in the same capacity in connection with the jurisdiction of justices of the peace.[1] In the sixteenth and seventeenth centuries these officials were variously known as borsholders, tithingmen, headboroughs, and thirdboroughs. This last term Lambard explains by asserting that in shires in which every third community had a constable the officers of the other two were called "third borrows," an explanation in which he is perhaps correct, notwithstanding the fact that he makes the usual error of identifying the *headborgh* with the borough.[2] When there were several headboroughs in one township or parish, only one of them acted as constable for the king, the others serving merely as manorial tithingmen.[3] Legal theory in the time of Lambard held that the justices of the peace had power to remove insufficient constables and borsholders and to appoint capable persons in their places,[4] — so far had the power of the justices undermined that of the leet. In some of the towns headboroughs continued to be appointed until 1835, serving as inspectors of weights and measures and in other minor capacities.[5] The tithingman without a tithing continued to act as a regular peace officer of the realm until 1839, when an act of Parliament left parochial constables the only ones to be appointed in the old way.[6] A further act of 1842 provided that "no petty constable, borsholder, tithingman,

---

[1] Lambard, *Constables*, 9; Simpson, "The Office of Constable," in *Eng. Hist. Review*, x. 625–641.

[2] Cox, *Derbyshire*, i. 109; Cox and Markham, *Records of Northampton*, i. 140–141. Cox's objection to the statement seems not to be well grounded, except as to the confusion of *borgh* with borough.

[3] Lambard, *Constables*, 9.

[4] *Ibid.* 18.

[5] Cox and Markham, *Records of Northampton*, ii. 142; Hudson, *Leet Jurisdiction in Norwich*, p. lxxiii.

[6] 2–3 Victoria, c. 93.

or peace officer of like description" should "be appointed for any parish, township, or vill within the limits of this act, except for the performance of duties unconnected with the preservation of the peace,"[1] and thus unequivocally took from this official duties which he had performed for more than seven centuries.

Finally, view of frankpledge as a name for the leet has been perpetuated to the present time, the jurisdiction sometimes existing in the nineteenth century in practically the same form as in the seventeenth.[2] Its functions have, however, been so far suspended by constabulary and local government acts that the mere name of an attenuated form of court is the last remaining relic of a system which once required all Englishmen of the lower classes to be in frankpledge suretyship.[3]

Frankpledge, with the arrangements for its maintenance, had in its day a profound influence in several directions. Viewed from the economic standpoint, it occasioned the collection of considerable sums of money from the peasants in addition to those which they already paid to their lords. It was, no doubt, on this ground that the Great Charter of 1217 fixed the sheriff's view of frankpledge after Michaelmas, when the crops were harvested and it was easiest to collect amercements and dues from the tillers of the soil. In addition to what went to the lord, the sheriff thus stepped in to claim some part of the harvest; or, if the lord held his own view of frankpledge, he took a larger share on this account.

The sums that were collected through the frankpledge system

---

[1] 5–6 Victoria, c. 109.

[2] See Crofton, *History of Newton Chapelry* (Chetham Soc.), ii. pt. i. 84. Hearnshaw (*Leet Jurisdiction in England*, 248–321) gives information concerning some 220 courts leet in England and Wales, nearly all of which were in existence in 1835.

[3] For an account of the court leet still held at Southampton, see Hearnshaw, *Leet Jurisdiction*, Introd.

in a given hundred year in and year out were considerable. The usual amercement of half a mark laid by the king's justices upon the tithing which had allowed a fugitive member to escape, or upon the township which had received a man without frank-pledge, came only at irregular intervals upon certain tithings and certain townships; but the penny collected from every man placed in frankpledge, and the payment at view of frank-pledge of at least a penny, sometimes of two pence, for every man in tithing, were regular features of the system. Further-more, the associates of the tithing seem ordinarily to have been required to pay an amercement for not attending the view in person, or else to make a regular payment in commutation of this duty, a plan which amounted to very much the same thing, though the sum paid under the latter arrangement was some-what smaller. Suit of tourn in the time of Edward I is the name not so much of a duty of the peasant as of a financial asset of the king. When, as often happened, the lord paid annually to the sheriff a sum varying usually from twenty to a very few shillings for the right of holding his view of frankpledge, the peasants were likely to be required to make up this amount to the lord. The lord, moreover, as well as the king, collected a sum fixed by custom "for frankpledge," a practice which, as has been observed, seems originally to have been justified on the ground that the money thus raised was required to meet the expense of holding the view. In the Staffordshire hundred of Seisdon in 1255 at least half of the tenants seem to have made such payments, the amounts here ranging from six pence up to six shillings and eight pence a year.[1] Sometimes the bailiff illegally exacted such a payment where it had not been made before,[2] or arbitrarily increased the usual amount,[3] as

---

[1] Salt Archaeol. Soc., *Collections*, v. pt. i. 110–116.
[2] See *Rot. Hundred.*, i. 486.   [3] *Ibid.* 138.

both he and the sheriff were tempted to do under the plan of farming hundreds and counties. Moreover, the capital pledge was subject to fine for certain irregularities on his part, varying in gravity from concealment of offences that ought to have been presented, or failure to have his men present when required, down to appearance before the dignified bailiff without removing his hat.[1]

The perquisites derived from view of frankpledge of course included all the amercements collected at the tourn for infraction of the peace in minor points or for violation of manorial usage. In a Staffordshire hundred in 1275 the amount of all such perquisites was estimated to be one hundred shillings a year.[2] In the thirteenth century the payments from view of frankpledge in eight hundreds in Warwickshire and Leicestershire made up almost forty-two pounds of the sheriff's annual ferm. In Hertfordshire a single hundred often paid from twenty to forty shillings. In Bedfordshire and Buckinghamshire together the amount from the same source aggregated almost forty pounds for one year.[3] When one adds to these payments various arbitrary and illegal exactions made upon the tithings and tithingmen in the time of Edward I, amounting sometimes to as much as one hundred shillings, it will readily be perceived that the frankpledge system oftentimes meant nothing less than a means of exploiting the peasants in the name of public peace.

Socially frankpledge was a mark of inferiority, except perhaps in the boroughs. It was, as has been seen, an instrument well adapted to enforce the servile obligations, and even the servile status, of the unfree manorial tenant. It was because

---

[1] See *Rot. Hundred.*, ii. 214.

[2] Salt Archaeol. Soc., *Collections*, vi. pt. i. 69.

[3] *Red Book of the Exchequer* (Rolls Series), ii. 775-777.

those who made up the tithings were usually villains that it was easy to make exactions of them, and to increase the obligations of the tithing and the tithingman until the load became excessively burdensome. The man in tithing had, however, one advantage: when he was accused of crime he could show that he was no vagrant,[1] and thus could claim whatever slight leniency was due him from this fact.[2] From the beginning of the early twelfth century, as Liebermann has well observed, legal competence depended on membership in frankpledge.[3] Even the despised approver might make appeals of felony, providing he was "one faithful and in frankpledge" and had a lord who would avow him.[4] The system at least bore testimony that a person had some sort of standing in the community.

 Judged from the collective rather than the individual point of view, frankpledge was an institution that helped to keep alive medieval local exclusiveness and to foster a narrow spirit of local selfishness. Attendance at the view of frankpledge for the hundred was not likely to take the peasant far from the manor; and when the lord held his own view the community, as Pollock and Maitland point out, rejoiced in the fact that "no tale went outside the manor to the ears of jealous neighbours or rapacious officials."[5] Such a protection of self-interest meant just the reverse of public spirit. The whole system was based on human selfishness. The tithing pursued its associate to avoid paying a fine; the capital pledge presented in court the offences of his neighbors for the same motive; and the whole community quickly reported the person who received a stranger on the manor, lest the newcomer commit an offence

[1] Maurer, *Saxon Mark Courts*, 32.
[2] See *Bracton's Note Book*, iii. 563; Salt Archaeol. Soc., *Collections*, iii. 43.
[3] Liebermann, *Ueber die Leges Edw. Conf.*, 82.
[4] Bracton, fol. 152, ii. 522.
[5] *English Law* (1895), i. 568.

and the vill be amerced for receiving him out of tithing. Under the practical continuance of this state of affairs through residency registration at the leet even after frankpledge itself was gone, there was thus a tendency toward that spirit of village selfishness which in the days of the Poor Laws often made against a new arrival a hypocritical accusation of moral unfitness for membership in the community, not because of any deep-seated regard for personal morality, but from a selfish fear lest some personal liability might arise through the newcomer's residence in the parish.

Against this disregard for the rights of the common man, and this fostering of local narrowness and selfishness, one has to set to the credit of the system political and constitutional results of a far better character. In an age of feudal confusion it was the agency through which the king claimed the direct allegiance of the great body of Englishmen. Frankpledge, moreover, at least after 1166, supplied the means of making men realize what that allegiance meant, by bringing the power of the king's government to bear directly on the individual. With all its imperfections considered as a constabulary system, with its clumsiness and disregard for the lower classes, frankpledge seems, nevertheless, to have secured in an effective manner the observance of the king's peace by the peasants of England, until at the end of the thirteenth century the plan failed because of a changed standard of economic values, as well as through its own tendency to emphasize the place of the capital pledge and through an inefficient system of gaol delivery. Even the money that was unequally exacted of the peasants through the institution went, not, like most of the other payments made by them, merely to add to seigniorial power, but usually to strengthen the royal hand, which could establish good government.

Considered from the constitutional point of view, the frankpledge system was an invaluable part of the framework of medieval English government. After the issue of the Assize of Clarendon and seigniorial imitation of the forms used in the sheriff's tourn, the view of frankpledge practically determined the mode of local administration followed by the greater part of the realm in town as well as in country.[1] Furthermore, as Stubbs shows, frankpledge constituted one form of representative system, the capital pledge and part of the tithing often assuming the old duty of the reeve and four in appearing for the township.[2] In this way the ordinary man became familiar with the workings both of the manorial and of the royal government of the county; for the tithings and the capital pledges appeared before the royal justices in eyre, as well as before the manorial steward, the bailiff of the hundred, or the sheriff of the shire. To quote Vinogradoff, frankpledge was in Norman days a " conspicuous link between both sections of society, . . . [connecting] the subjugated population with the hundred court, which is the starting-point of free judicial organisation."[3] It was, therefore, in no small degree due to the operation of the system of frankpledge that the masses of the English people learned not only how to carry on their own local affairs, but also how to aid the king's officers in the royal government of the shires. Such acquaintance of the masses with matters of administration and justice, and especially such participation in them, have made possible Anglo-Saxon self-government.

---

[1] In the sixteenth century the court leet not only enforced police regulations in towns, but also actually made such regulations. Thus in 1592 the jurors at Bermondsey in Surrey present that there be "no casting forth of dust or soil on Saturday afternoon by the inhabitants of Bell alley " (Public Record Office, Court Rolls, Bundle 126, No. 1868 C). At Southwark in 1658 general orders and by-laws appear to have been made in the same way (see British Museum, Additional Charter, No. 36793, fol. 17).

[2] *Constitutional History*, i. 95.   [3] *Villainage*, 66.

APPENDICES

APPENDICES

APPENDIX A

ROYAL WRIT FOR HOLDING VIEW OF FRANKPLEDGE, 1218[1]

De atachiamentis pertinentibus ad coronam, et aliis. Rex omnibus militibus, libere tenentibus et aliis de hundredo de Ferendon, salutem. Mandamus vobis, firmiter precipientes, quod, sicut vos et omnia vestra diligitis, veniatis ad diem et ad locum vobis assignatos a vicecomite nostro Berkesire, ad ostendendum eidem vicecomiti, ad turnum suum, placita et attachiamenta, que pertinent ad coronam nostram, coram coronatoribus comitatus ejusdem ad hoc assignatis; et ad ostendendum eidem vicecomiti visum franci plegii secundum quod fieri solet temporibus H. regis, avi nostri, et R. regis, avunculi nostri, et J. regis, patris nostri. Et in hujus etc. Teste comite, apud Farendon, vj. die Marcii, anno regni nostri secundo.

Eodem modo scribitur omnibus etc. de hundredo de Waneting, et omnibus etc. de hundredo de Lamburn.

APPENDIX B

OATH OF PERSONS PUT UNDER FRANKPLEDGE IN LONDON, FOURTEENTH CENTURY[2]

Serement de ceux qi serrount mys dessouz Franc Plegge.

Vous jurrez qe vous serrez foialx et loialx au Roy d'Engleterre et a sez heires, Rois, et la peas du Roi garderez; et as ministres de la citee obeisante serrez, et as toutz heurez, qe mestiere soit, prestez

---

[1] *Patent Rolls of the Reign of Henry III*, 1216–1225, p. 141.
[2] *Liber Albus* (ed. Riley, Rolls Series), i. 315.

serrez deydere lez ministres darrester lez meffesours et disobeysantes
a la pees le Roi, sibien privez come estraunges. Et prestz serrez, al
garnissement dez Conestables et Bedelles, pur faire lez gaytes et
autres charges pur la sauf garde de la peas, et toutz lez poyntz en cest
Wardemot monstrez, solonc vostre poiare bien et loialment tendrez.
Et si savez ascun male covyne deinz la Garde ou la citee, vous le
destourbrez ou a vostre Alderman assavoir ferrez — si Dieu vous
eide, et lez Seintz.

APPENDIX C

TITHING-LIST AT HARSTON, CAMBRIDGESHIRE, IN THE REIGN OF RICHARD II [1]

Hardeleston
Capitales plegii cum decenariis

JOHANNES BOLE

Johannes Aleyne
Johannes Baldewyne
~~Johannes Reynald~~ quia mortuus [2]
Thomas Willesson
*Nicholaus Alnene [3]
~~Willelmus Reynald~~ quia mortuus
Johannes filius Thome Taillour
Johannes Walssheman
*Johannes Aleyne junior mortuus est
~~Johannes Strong~~ quia mortuus
~~Rogerus filius Thome Adam~~ amotus
propter festum, ijd.
~~Johannes Smyth~~
Johannes filius Ricardi Wrighte
*Johannes filius Johannis Cokkeshed
Johannes Toteneye
~~Johannes Dun~~
Johannes Coupere
~~Henricus Merymouth~~ quia mortuus

[1] British Museum, Additional Charter, No. 18526.
[2] In the manuscript such words are written above the name.
[3] The asterisks are in the original list, but their meaning is not apparent.

mortuus est
~~JOHANNES COKKESHED~~

WILLELMUS LUCAS

Johannes Strong quia mortuus
Johannes Lucas clerk
~~Thomas Alnene~~ quia mortuus
Thomas Tepelyn
Robertus Tepelyn mortuus est
Johannes Bangil Shepherd
*Johannes filius Johannis clerk
~~Thomas filius Radulphi Walssheman~~ quia
mortuus est
*Johannes Pycard Junior
Johannes filius Johannis Wryghte
~~Johannes Hygyn~~
Johannes Walssheman junior
*Augustinus Wyltons junior
Johannes Lucas
~~Johannes Warde~~ quia mortuus
~~Willelmus Lucas~~ quia capitalis plegius

JOHANNES PYCARD

~~Willelmus Taylour~~ quia mortuus
~~Johannes Godyng~~

JOHANNES WRIGHTE
mortuus Wright
JOHANNES BOLE

Willelmus Dun
Johannes filius Roberti de Bery
~~Robertus de Bery~~ quia mortuus
~~Johannes Prat~~
Willelmus Everesdon mortuus est
Thomas Prat
Thomas Warde
Thomas Ricard quia mortuus

JOHANNES GODYNG

Johannes filius Willelmi Godyng quia
mortuus

mortuus

NIGELLUS STURTUGGA   ~~Johannes Godyng~~ quia mortuus
Johannes Say

ROBERTUS LUCAS   Willelmus filius Roberti Godyng
Johannes Urney junior mortuus est
Augustinus Godyng
Thomas Lucas
Willelmus Rycard mortuus est
~~Willelmus Dassh~~ quia mortuus
~~Willelmus Rylene~~ amotus propter festum
Willelmus Lucas

APPENDIX D

LIST OF WORKS CITED

ADAMS, G. B.   Henry I's writ regarding the local courts. *American Historical Review*, viii. 487–490.   New York, etc., 1903.
——   History of England from the Norman Conquest to the death of John.   London, etc., 1905.

ANGLO-SAXON chronicle, with a translation.   Edited by Benjamin Thorpe.   Rolls Series.   2 vols.   London, 1861.

ANNALES monastici.   Edited by H. R. Luard.   Rolls Series.   5 vols. London, 1864–1869.

ASSIZE rolls.   MSS. in Public Record Office.

ATKYNS, ROBERT.   The ancient and present state of Gloucestershire. 2d edition.   London, 1768.

BACON, NATHANIEL.   Historical discourse of the uniformity of the government of England.   London, 1647–1651.

BAIGENT, F. J., editor.   Collection of records and documents relating to the hundred and manor of Crondal.   Hampshire Record Society.   London, etc., 1891.

BAILDON, W. P., editor.   Court rolls of the manor of Wakefield. Yorkshire Archaeol. Society, *Record Series*, Vols. xxix, xxxvi. [Worksop], 1901, 1906.

BATESON, MARY, editor. Borough customs. Selden Society. 2
vols. London, 1904-1906.
—— Records of the borough of Leicester. 3 vols. London,
1899-1905.
BEARD, CHARLES A. The office of justice of the peace in England
in its origin and development. Columbia University, *Studies
in History, Economics, and Public Law*, Vol. xx, No. 1. New
York, 1904.
BICKLEY, F. B., editor. Extracts from the court rolls of the manor
of Dulwich, 1333-1693. Young's *History of Dulwich College*,
ii. 266-320. London, etc., 1889.
BLACK book of the admiralty (Monumenta Juridica). Edited by
Sir Travers Twiss. Roll Series. 4 vols. London, 1871-1876.
BOLDON buke: a survey of the possessions of the see of Durham
made by order of Bishop Hugh Pudsey in 1183, with a transla-
tion. Edited by William Greenwell. Surtees Society. Dur-
ham, 1852.
BOULTER, W. C., editor. Court rolls of some East Riding manors,
1563-1573. *Yorkshire Archaeol. and Topog. Journal*, x. 63-82.
London, 1889.
BRACTON, HENRY DE. Henrici de Bracton De legibus et consuetudin-
ibus Angliae libri quinque. Edited by Sir Travers Twiss.
Rolls Series. 6 vols. London, 1878-1883.
BRACTON's note book. Edited by F. W. Maitland. 3 vols. London,
1887.
BRAKELOND, JOCELIN DE. Chronica Jocelini de Brakelonda de
rebus gestis Samsonis abbatis monasterii Sancti Edmundi, nunc
primum typis mandata curante J. G. Rokewode. Camden
Society. London, 1840.
BRITISH MUSEUM MSS. Additional charters, Nos. 18526 and
36793.
BRITTON: the French text carefully revised, with an English translation. Edited by F. M. Nichols. 2 vols. Oxford, 1865.
BROWN, WILLIAM, editor. Yorkshire inquisitions. Yorkshire Archaeol.
and Topog. Assoc., *Record Series*, Vol. xii. [Worksop], 1892.
CALENDAR of the charter rolls preserved in the Public Record Office.
3 vols. London, 1903-1908.

CALENDAR of the justiciary rolls, or the proceedings in the court of the justiciar of Ireland. Edited by James Mills. Dublin, 1905.

CALENDAR of the muniments of the borough of Shrewsbury. Shrewsbury, 1896.

CALENDAR of the patent rolls, A. D. 1216, etc. London, 1891, etc.

CARDIFF records. Edited by J. H. Matthews. 5 vols. Cardiff, 1898-1905.

CARTULARIUM abbathiae de Rievalle. [Edited by J. C. Atkinson.] Surtees Society. Durham, etc., 1889.

CARTULARIUM abbathiae de Whiteby. [Edited by J. C. Atkinson.] Surtees Society. 2 vols. Durham, etc., 1879-1881.

CARTULARIUM monasterii de Rameseia. Edited by W. H. Hart and P. A. Lyons. Rolls Series. 3 vols. London, 1884-1893.

CARTULARIUM monasterii S. Petri Gloucestriae (Historia et). Edited by W. H. Hart. Rolls series. 3 vols. London, 1863-1867.

CHARTULARY of Cockersand Abbey. See FARRER, WILLIAM.

CHESTER eyre and quo warranto rolls. MSS. in Public Record Office.

CHEYNEY, EDWARD P. The disappearance of English serfdom. *English Historical Review,* xv. 20-37. London, etc., 1900.

CHRONICON monasterii de Abingdon. Edited by Joseph Stevenson. Rolls Series. 2 vols. London, 1858.

CHRONICON monasterii S. Albani. Edited by H. T. Riley. Rolls Series. 12 vols. London, 1863-1876.

CLARK, ANDREW. Serfdom on an Essex manor, 1308-1378. *English Historical Review,* xx. 479-483. London, etc., 1905.

—— Tithing lists from Essex. *Ibid.* xix. 715-719.

CLARK, GEORGE T., editor. The custumary of the manor and soke of Rothley in the county of Leicester. *Archaeologia,* xlvii. pt. i. 89-130. London, 1882.

CODEX diplomaticus aevi Saxonici. Edited by J. M. Kemble. English Historical Society. 6 vols. London, 1839-1848.

COKE, EDWARD. The second part of the institutes of the laws of England. 4th edition. London, 1671.

COOTE, H. C. The Romans of Britain. London, 1878.

CORAM rege rolls, Nos. 118 and 125. MSS. in Public Record Office.

COURT rolls. MSS. in Public Record Office.

COURT rolls of stannaries. MSS. in Public Record Office.

COX, J. C. Three centuries of Derbyshire annals as illustrated by the records of the quarter sessions of the county of Derby. 2 vols. London, 1890.

COX, J. C., and MARKHAM, C. A., editors. Records of the borough of Northampton. Northampton, etc., 1898.

CROFTON, Henry T. Folk-moots of Lancashire and Cheshire. Lancashire and Cheshire Antiquarian Society, *Transactions,* v. 117–145. Manchester, 1888.

—— History of Newton chapelry in the ancient parish of Manchester. Chetham Society. 3 vols. in 4. [London], 1904–1905.

DALLAWAY, JAMES. A history of the western division of the county of Sussex, including the rapes of Chichester, Arundel, and Bramber, with the city and diocese of Chichester. 2 vols. in 3 pts. London, 1815–1830.

DAVIES, J. S. A history of Southampton. Southampton, etc., 1883.

DAVIS, H. W. C. A review of Ueber das Englische Rechtsbuch 'Leges Henrici' by Liebermann. *English Historical Review,* xvii. 147–149. London, 1902.

—— The liberties of Bury St. Edmunds. *Ibid.* xxiv. 417–431.

DRAKE, HENRY H., editor. Hasted's History of Kent: Part i, Blackheath hundred. London, 1886.

DUGDALE, WILLIAM. The antiquities of Warwickshire. 2d edition, revised. 2 vols. London, 1730.

—— Monasticon Anglicanum. Edited by John Caley and others. 6 vols. in 8. London, 1817–1830.

DUNCUMB, JOHN. Collections towards the history and antiquities of Hereford. 3 vols. (Vol. iii. by W. H. Cooke.) Hereford, etc., 1804–1882. — Continuations by W. H. Cooke, London, 1892; and M. G. Watkins, Hereford, 1897.

EYTON, R. W. The antiquities of Shropshire. 12 vols. London, 1854–1860.

FARRER, WILLIAM, editor. The chartulary of Cockersand Abbey, of the Premonstratensian order. Chetham Society. 3 vols. in 6 pts. [Manchester], 1898–1905.

—— The Lancashire pipe rolls of 31 Henry I, A. D. 1130; and of the reigns of Henry II, Richard I, and King John. Liverpool, 1902.

FEUDAL AIDS. Inquisitions and assessments relating to feudal aids, with analogous documents preserved in the Public Record Office, 1284–1431. 5 vols. London, 1899–1908.

FINLASON, W. F. Introduction to [John] Reeves's History of the English law from the time of the Romans to the end of the reign of Elizabeth. 3 vols. London, 1869.

FITZHERBERT, ANTHONY. La graunde abridgement. n. p., 1565.

FLETA, seu commentarius juris Anglicani. 2d edition. London, 1685.

GAGE, JOHN. The history and antiquities of Suffolk: Thingoe hundred. London, 1838.

[GALE, ROGER, editor.] Registrum honoris de Richmond. London, 1722.

GESTA abbatum monasterii S. Albani. See RILEY, H. T.

GNEIST, RUDOLF. Das Englische Verwaltungsrecht. 2 vols. Berlin, 1867.

—— History of the English constitution. Translated by P. A. Ashworth. London, 1891.

GREEN, JOHN RICHARD. The conquest of England. [Edited by Alice Stopford Green.] London, 1883.

GRIFFITH, EDWARD. Collection of ancient records relating to the borough of Huntingdon. London, 1827.

GROSS, CHARLES. The gild merchant. 2 vols. Oxford, 1890.

—— Select cases from the coroners' rolls. Selden Society. London, 1896.

HARLAND, JOHN, editor. Mamecestre: being chapters from the early recorded history of the barony, the lordship or manor, the vill, borough, or town of Manchester. Chetham Society. 3 vols. [Manchester], 1861–1862.

—— A volume of court leet records of the manor of Manchester. Chetham Society. [Manchester], 1864.

HARROD, HENRY. Calendar of the court rolls of the borough of Colchester. Colchester, [1865].

HEALEY, C. E. H. C., editor. Somersetshire pleas (civil and criminal) from the rolls of the itinerant justices. Somerset Record Society, [*Publications*], Vol. xi. [London], 1897.

HEARNSHAW, F. J. C. Leet jurisdiction in England, especially as illustrated by the records of the court leet of Southampton. Southampton Record Society. Southampton, 1908.

—— Southampton court leet records. Southampton Record Society. 1 vol. in 2 pts. Southampton, 1905–1906.

HEDGES, J. K. The history of Wallingford. 2 vols. London, 1881.

HERVEY, LORD JOHN, editor. The hundred rolls and extracts therefrom, with a translation: county of Suffolk. Ipswich, 1902.

HONE, NATHANIEL J., editor. The manor and manorial records. London, [1906].

HOVEDEN, ROGER OF. Chronica Rogeri de Houedene. Edited by William Stubbs. Rolls Series. 4 vols. London, 1868–1871.

HOWARD, GEORGE ELLIOTT. On the development of the king's peace and the English local peace-magistracy. University of Nebraska, *University Studies*, i. 235–299. Lincoln, Neb., 1890.

HUDSON, WILLIAM, editor. Leet jurisdiction in the city of Norwich during the thirteenth and fourteenth centuries. Selden Society. London, 1892.

HUNDRED rolls. See ROTULI HUNDREDORUM.

—— The hundred rolls and extracts therefrom, with a translation by the late Lord John Hervey: county of Suffolk. Ipswich, 1902.

INNES, COSMO, editor. Ancient laws and customs of the burghs of Scotland. Edinburgh, 1868.

INQUISITIONES post mortem for the county of Worcester. See WILLIS-BUND, J. W.

INQUISITIONES post mortem for Wiltshire. See WILTSHIRE.

JACKSON, J. E., translator. The sheriff's tourn, co. Wilts, A. D. 1439. *Wiltshire Archaeol. and Nat. Hist. Magazine*, xiii. 105–118. Devizes, etc., 1872.

JESSOPP, AUGUSTUS. The coming of the friars, and other historic essays. 4th edition. London, 1890.

KEMBLE, J. M. The Saxons in England. 2 vols. London, 1849.

KITCHIN, G. W., editor. Charter of Edward III confirming and enlarging the privileges of St. Giles Fair, Winchester, 1349. [Hampshire Record Society.] London, etc., 1886.

—— The manor of Manydown. Hampshire Record Society. London, etc., 1895.

KITCHIN, JOHN. Le court leete et court baron. London, 1580.

LAMBARD, WILLIAM. Duties of constables, borsholders, tythingmen, and such other lowe and lay ministers of the peace. London, 1599.

LANCASHIRE AND CHESHIRE ANTIQUARIAN SOCIETY. Transactions, 1883, etc. Manchester, 1884, etc.

LANCASHIRE AND CHESHIRE RECORD SOCIETY. [Publications. London], 1879, etc.

LAPSLEY, G. T. The county palatine of Durham: a study in constitutional history. New York, etc., 1900.

—— The problem of the north. *American Historical Review*, v. 440–466. New York, etc., 1900.

LEWIS, HUBERT. Ancient laws of Wales. London, 1889.

LIBER albus. See RILEY, H. T.

LIBER custumarum. See RILEY, H. T.

LIEBERMANN, FELIX. Consiliatio Cnuti. Halle, 1893.

—— Die Gesetze der Angelsachsen. Vols. i–ii. pt. i. Halle, 1898–1906.

—— Einleitung zum Statut der Londoner Friedensgilde unter Aethelstan. *Mélanges Fitting*, ii. 79–103. Montpellier, 1908.

—— Ueber die Leges Anglorum saeculo xiii ineunte Londoniis collectae. Halle, 1894.

—— Ueber die Leges Edwardi Confessoris. Halle, 1896.

LIST of sheriffs for England and Wales. See PUBLIC RECORD OFFICE.

MADOX, THOMAS. Firma burgi, or an historical essay concerning the cities and boroughs of England. London, 1726.

—— History and antiquity of the exchequer of England. 2d edition. 2 vols. London, 1769.

MAITLAND, F. W. Domesday book and beyond: three essays on the early history of England. Cambridge, 1897.

—— Pleas of the crown for the county of Gloucester. London, 1884.

—— Select pleas in manorial and other seignorial courts. Vol. i. Selden Society. London, 1889.

—— Select pleas of the crown. Vol. i. Selden Society. London, 1888.

MAITLAND, F. W., and BAILDON, W. P., editors. The court baron, together with select pleas from the bishop of Ely's court of Littleport. Selden Society. London, 1891.

MALMESBURY, WILLIAM OF. De gestis regum Anglorum libri quinque. Edited by William Stubbs. Rolls Series. 2 vols. London, 1887–1889.

MANCHESTER. See HARLAND, JOHN.

MANDLEY, J. G. DE T., editor. The portmote or court leet records of the borough or town and royal manor of Salford, from 1597 to 1669. Chetham Society. 2 vols. [Manchester], 1902.

MARKHAM, C. A., and COX, J. C., editors. Records of the borough of Northampton. Northampton, etc., 1898.

MARQUARDSEN, HEINRICH. Ueber Haft und Bürgschaft bei den Angelsachsen. Erlangen, 1852.

MARSH, A. E. W. History of the borough and town of Calne. Calne, etc., 1904.

MAURER, KONRAD. Angelsächsische Rechtsverhältnisse. *Kritische Ueberschau der Deutschen Gesetzgebung*, i. 47–120, 405–431; ii. 30–68, 388–440; iii. 26–61. Munich, 1853–1856.

MAURER, WILLIAM. An inquiry into Anglo-Saxon mark-courts. London, etc., 1855.

MAYO, C. H. The municipal records of the borough of Shaftesbury. Sherborne, 1889.

MEREWETHER, H. A., and STEPHENS, A. J. History of the boroughs and municipal corporations of the United Kingdom. 3 vols. London, 1835.

MIRROR of justices. Edited by W. J. Whittaker. Selden Society. London, 1895.

MONTACUTE. See TWO CARTULARIES.

NICHOLS, F. M. Original documents illustrative of the administration of the criminal law in the time of Edward I. *Archaeologia*, xl. pt. i. 89–105.

NORTH RIDING RECORD SOCIETY. [Publications.] 13 vols. London, 1884–1897. 1st Series, Quarter sessions records (ed. J. C. Atkinson), 9 vols.; New Series, The honor and forest of Pickering (ed. R. B. Turton), 4 vols.

NORTHUMBERLAND assize rolls. See PAGE, WILLIAM.

OGLE, OCTAVIUS, editor. Royal letters addressed to Oxford and now existing in the city archives. Oxford, 1892.

ORMEROD, GEORGE. History of the county palatine, and city of Chester. 2nd edition, by Thomas Helsby. 3 vols. London, 1882.

PAGE, WILLIAM. Some remarks on the Northumbrian palatinates and regalities. *Archaeologia*, li. pt. i. 143–155. London, 1888.

—— Three early assize rolls for the county of Northumberland. Surtees Society. Durham, etc., 1891.

—— The Victoria history of Lancashire. Vol. i. London, 1906.

PALGRAVE, FRANCIS. The rise and progress of the English commonwealth. 2 vols. London, 1832.

PARKER, JOHN, editor. Calendar of the Lancashire assize rolls. Record Society for Lancashire and Cheshire. 2 pts. [London], 1904–1905.

PARLIAMENTARY writs. Edited by Francis Palgrave. Record Commission. 2 vols. in 4. [London], 1827–1834.

PIPE ROLLS. The great roll of the pipe for the first year of the reign of King Richard the First. Edited by Joseph Hunter. London, 1884.

—— The great rolls of the pipe, 5–26 Henry II. Pipe Roll Society. 29 vols. London, 1884–1908.

—— The great rolls of the Pipe, 24 Henry II to 10 Richard I. MSS. in Public Record Office.

—— The pipe-rolls, or sheriff's annual accounts of the revenues of the crown for the counties of Cumberland, Westmorland, and Durham. Society of Antiquaries of Newcastle-upon-Tyne. Newcastle, 1847.

PLACITA de quo warranto, Edward I to Edward III. [Edited by William Illingworth.] Record Commission. [London], 1818.

PLACITORUM in domo capitulari Westmonasteriensi asservatorum abbrevatio. Record Commission. [London], 1811.

POLLOCK, SIR FREDERICK, and MAITLAND, F. W. History of English law before the time of Edward I. 2 vols. Cambridge, 1895.

POOLE, REGINALD LANE, editor. Historical atlas of modern Europe. Oxford, 1902.

POWELL, ROBERT. Antiquity, authority, uses, and jurisdiction of the ancient courts of leet or view of frankpledge. London, 1642.

PUBLIC RECORD OFFICE. List of sheriffs for England and Wales [to 1831]. Public Record Office, *Lists and Indexes*, No. ix. London, 1898.

—— MSS.: assize rolls, coram rege rolls, court rolls, court rolls of stannaries, pipe rolls, and Chester eyre and quo warranto rolls.

RAINE, JAMES. The history and antiquities of North Durham. London, 1852.

RAMSAY, JAMES H. The foundations of England. 2 vols. London, 1898.

RECORD OF CAERNARVON. Registrum vulgariter nuncupatur "The Record of Caernarvon." [Edited by Sir Henry Ellis.] Record Commission. [London], 1838.

RED book of the exchequer. Edited by Hubert Hall. Rolls Series. 3 vols. London, 1896.

REGISTER of S. Osmund. Edited by W. H. R. Jones. Rolls Series. 2 vols. London, 1883-1884.

RILEY, H. T., editor. Gesta abbatum monasterii S. Albani a Thoma Walsingham [A. D. 793-1401]. Rolls Series. 3 vols. London, 1867-1869.

—— Munimenta gildhallae Londoniensis: Liber albus, Liber custumarum, et Liber Horn. Rolls Series. 3 vols. London, 1859-1862.

ROGERS, J. E. T., editor. Oxford city documents, financial and judicial, 1268-1665. Oxford Historical Society. Oxford, 1891.

ROTULI chartarum in Turri Londoniensi asservati. Edited by Thomas Duffus Hardy. Record Commission. [London], 1837.

ROTULI curiae regis. Edited by Sir Francis Palgrave. Record Commission. 2 vols. [London], 1835.

ROTULI hundredorum, temp. Henry III et Edward I. Record Commission. 2 vols. [London], 1812-1818.

ROTULI parliamentorum [1278-1503]. 6 vols. n.p. n.d.—Index, 1832.

RYE, WALTER. Notes on crime and accident in Norfolk, temp. Edward I (extracts from gaol-delivery rolls, 14 Edward I). *Archaeological Review*, ii. 201-215. London, 1889.

—— Some rough materials for a history of the hundred of North Erpingham. 3 pts. Norwich, 1883-1889.

SALT (WILLIAM) ARCHAEOLOGICAL SOCIETY. Collections for a

history of Staffordshire. 18 vols. Birmingham, 1880–1897. New series, 1898, etc.

SCARGILL-BIRD, S. R., editor. Custumals of Battle abbey, in the reigns of Edward I and Edward II. Camden Society. [London], 1887.

SCHMID, REINHOLD, editor. Die Gesetze der Angelsachsen. Leipsic, 1858.

SHARPE, R. R., editor. Calendar of the letter-books of the city of London, A. D. 1275, etc. London, 1899, etc.

SHROPSHIRE ARCHAEOLOGICAL AND NATURAL HISTORY SOCIETY. Transactions. Shrewsbury, 1878 (1877), etc.

SIMPSON, H. B. The office of constable. *English Historical Review*, x. 625–641. London, etc., 1895.

SMITH, LUCY T., editor. A common-place book of the fifteenth century. London, etc., 1886.

SMITH, SIR THOMAS. The common-welth of England, and maner of government thereof. London, 1589.

SOMERSETSHIRE pleas. See HEALEY, C. E. H. C.

STATUTES. 2d revised edition, 1235–1886. 16 vols. London, 1888–1900.

—— Statutes of the realm. Edited by A. Luders, T. E. Tomlins, J. Raithby, and others. Record Commission. 11 vols. [London, 1810–1828.]

[STEVENSON, W. H., editor.] Records of the borough of Nottingham. 5 vols. (Vol. v. by W. T. Baker.) London and Nottingham, 1882–1900.

STOW, JOHN. A survey of the cities of London and Westminster and the borough of Southwark. London, 1633.

STUBBS, WILLIAM. The constitutional history of England. 3 vols. Oxford, 1897, 1896, 1903. — Vol. i is 6th ed.; vol. ii, 5th; vol. iii, 4th.

—— Select charters and other illustrations of English constitutional history. 8th edition. Oxford, 1900.

SURTEES, ROBERT. History and antiquities of the county palatine of Durham. 4 vols. London, etc., 1816–1840.

TAIT, JAMES. Medieval Manchester and the beginnings of Lancashire. Manchester, 1904.

THORPE, BENJAMIN, editor. Ancient laws and institutes of England. Record Commission. 2 vols. [London], 1840.

TURNER, G. J., editor. Select pleas of the forest, 10 John to 8 Edward III. Selden Society. London, 1901.

TURTON, ROBERT B., editor. The honor and forest of Pickering. North Riding Record Society, [*Publications*], New Series. 4 vols. London, 1894–1897.

Two cartularies of the Augustinian priory of Bruton and the Cluniac priory of Montacute. Edited by various hands. Somerset Record Society, [*Publications*], Vol. viii. [London], 1894.

VICTORIA history of the county of Cumberland. Edited by James Wilson. 2 vols. Westminster, 1901–1905.

—— Victoria history of Lancashire. See PAGE, WILLIAM.

VINOGRADOFF, PAUL. English society in the eleventh century: essays in English mediaeval history. Oxford, 1908.

—— The growth of the manor. London, etc., 1905.

—— Villainage in England: essays in English mediaeval history. Oxford, 1892.

WAITZ, GEORGE. Deutsche Verfassungsgeschichte. 2d edition. 6 vols. Kiel, etc., 1865–1896.

WALBRAN, J. R., editor. Memorials of the abbey of St. Mary of Fountains. Surtees Society. 2 vols. Durham, etc., 1863–1878.

WATSON, EDWARD J., editor. Pleas of the crown for the hundred of Swineshead and the township of Bristol. Bristol, 1902.

WILLIS-BUND, J. W., editor. Inquisitiones post mortem for the county of Worcester. Worcestershire Historical Society. Pt. i. Oxford, 1894.

—— Worcester county records: calendar of the quarter sessions. Worcestershire Historical Society. 2 pts. Worcester, 1899–1900.

WILTSHIRE ARCHAEOLOGICAL AND NATURAL HISTORY SOCIETY. Abstracts of the inquisitiones post mortem relating to Wiltshire, from the reign of Henry III. Vol. i, in 7 pts. [Devizes], 1902–1908.

—— Magazine. Devizes, 1854, etc.

WRIGHT, THOMAS, editor. Anglo-Saxon and old English vocabularies. 2d edition, by R. P. Wülcker. 2 vols. London, 1884.

[YEAR BOOKS]. Les reports des cases [Edward II to 27 Henry VIII]. 11 pts. London, 1678–1680.

—— Year books of the reign of Edward I. Edited by A. J. Horwood. Rolls Series. 5 vols. London, 1866–1879.

YEATMAN, J. P. The feudal history of the county of Derby. 5 vols. in 9 sections. London, etc., [1886–1907].

YORKSHIRE ARCHAEOLOGICAL AND TOPOGRAPHICAL ASSOCIATION (since 1893 called Yorkshire Archaeological Society). Journal. London, 1870, etc.

—— Record series. [Worksop], 1885, etc.

YOUNG, WILLIAM. History of Dulwich College. 2 vols. London, etc., 1889.

INDEX

INDEX